# OPEN THE BIBLE
# IN 30 DAYS

# OPEN THE BIBLE IN 30 DAYS

## COLIN S. SMITH

MOODY PUBLISHERS

CHICAGO

All Scripture quotations are taken from the Holy Bible, New International Version®, NIV®. Copyright © 1973, 1978, 1984, 2011 by Biblica, Inc.™ Used by permission of Zondervan. All rights reserved worldwide. www.zondervan.com. The "NIV" and "New International Version" are trademarks registered in the United States Patent and Trademark Office by Biblica, Inc.™

Scripture quotations marked NASB taken from the New American Standard Bible® (NASB), Copyright © 1960, 1962, 1963, 1968, 1971, 1972, 1973, 1975, 1977, 1995 by The Lockman Foundation. Used by permission. www.Lockman.org

Scripture quotations marked (ESV) are from the ESV® Bible (The Holy Bible, English Standard Version®), copyright © 2001 by Crossway, a publishing ministry of Good News Publishers. Used by permission. All rights reserved.

Published in association with the literary agency of Wolgemuth & Associates.

Edited by Jim Vincent and Kevin P. Emmert
Interior and cover design: Erik M. Peterson

All websites and phone numbers listed herein are accurate at the time of publication but may change in the future or cease to exist. The listing of website references and resources does not imply publisher endorsement of the site's entire contents. Groups and organizations are listed for informational purposes, and listing does not imply publisher endorsement of their activities.

ISBN: 978-0-8024-2344-3

Originally delivered by fleets of horse-drawn wagons, the affordable paperbacks from D. L. Moody's publishing house resourced the church and served everyday people. Now, after more than 125 years of publishing and ministry, Moody Publishers' mission remains the same—even if our delivery systems have changed a bit. For more information on other books (and resources) created from a biblical perspective, go to www.moodypublishers.com or write to:

Moody Publishers
820 N. LaSalle Boulevard
Chicago, IL 60610

1 3 5 7 9 10 8 6 4 2

*Printed in the United States of America*

*TO A. J.,*
*WHOSE LIGHT IS STILL SHINING*

# Contents

## PART THREE: LIVING IN THE SPIRIT

*Introduction*

**YOU ARE ABOUT TO EMBARK** on a fascinating journey as we travel together through the Bible story. You will discover who God is and what He is doing in the world. You will also learn about yourself and God's purpose for your life.

The Bible unveils the amazing story of how God has reached out to this rebel world, offering a relationship with Himself to all people. It explains why life in this world is such a confusing mixture of pain and pleasure, and it tells how God offers to bring us into a life of unclouded joy.

I find it helpful to think of the Bible story as a magnificent landscape of high mountains and deep valleys. We will climb its mountains of triumph and explore its valleys of disaster. Along the way, we will meet extraordinary people whose experiences of faith, fear, high hopes, and broken dreams cover the whole of life. We will encounter the entire range of human emotions—from love to hate and from dread to joy.

The first stage of our journey will take us through the Old Testament, where God introduces Himself to us. He made Himself known in five spectacular bursts of activity. But between these great mountaintops were long, dark valleys, where God seemed to be distant, and where the power of evil seemed overwhelming.

The second stage of our journey will take us through the Gospels, where we meet Jesus Christ. We will focus on six towering peaks where His glory is seen most clearly, but we will also enter His pain and suffering as we travel with Him through the darkest valleys.

The last stage of our journey will take us through the letters of the New Testament, where we discover the joys and struggles of life in the Spirit. The Christian life has its mountaintops and its valleys, and through our journey, you will become familiar with both.

*Open the Bible in 30 Days* includes a short study guide that will help you apply the truths you have learned. You can use its questions on your own or as part of a study group sharing the thirty-day journey together.

Once you have breathed the air of the mountains, you will want to come back for more. And you can find more at openthebible.org, where you will discover an expanded journey through the Bible story.

That's the plan for the journey. Now it's time to break camp and head for the mountains.

# PART ONE

# Knowing God
*the Father*

| Adam/Eve | 2000 BC<br>Abraham/Isaac/Jacob | 1500 BC<br>Moses/Joshua |
|---|---|---|

**CREATION**     **PROMISE**     **COVENANT**

**CURSE**     **PAIN**

| 1000 BC | 500 BC | *Birth of* |
| David/Solomon | Ezra/Nehemiah | *Jesus Christ* |

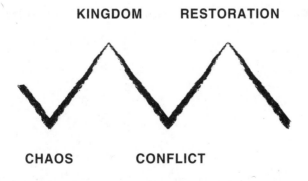

**KINGDOM**   **RESTORATION**

**CHAOS**   **CONFLICT**

**THE OLD TESTAMENT STORY** takes us from the beginning of time to about the year 400 BC.

The main events cluster around five grand occasions when God intercepted human history in a spectacular way. They are

1. God's gift of life in creation,
2. God's promise to Abraham,
3. God's covenant with His people,
4. God's kingdom under David and Solomon, and
5. God's restoration of His people from exile.

Between these five mountain peaks of God's intervention lie four deep valleys. They are

1. the curse that followed the entrance of sin into the world,
2. the pain God's people endured as slaves in Egypt,
3. the chaos God's people experienced in the Promised Land, and
4. the conflict that led to exile in Babylon.

Once you have explored these mountains and valleys, you will have a good grasp of the Old Testament story and, more important, you will have discovered who God is and what He has to say to you.

*Chapter 1*

---

# creation

**HOW COULD ANYONE** possibly know how the world began? Nobody was there taking notes when it happened! And how could anyone know what was in the mind of God when He made the first man and woman? No one could know these things unless God Himself took the initiative to tell somebody. And that is precisely what He did.

We can reasonably assume that God spoke with Adam and Eve about His joy in creating the universe and that they passed these stories on to their children. But stories that are handed down from generation to generation in this way become distorted, and so it is important to realize that God revealed these things more directly.

Later in our journey, we will meet with Moses. God appeared to him visibly and spoke to him audibly (see Num. 12:8). This unique privilege of speaking with God face-to-face enabled Moses to write what God gave him to say in the first five books of the Bible.

## THE CREATOR IS THE OWNER

The first thing God wants you to know is that He is your Creator: "In the beginning God created the heavens and the earth" (Gen. 1:1). That's important, because a creator always has the rights of ownership over anything that he or she has made. God wants you to know that He is the Creator and therefore the owner of everything, including you.

That tells you something magnificent, not only about God but also about you. You are not an accident of history whose existence is the result of certain atoms colliding by random chance. God made you on purpose, and you will discover that purpose as you come to know Him.

## A BREATHTAKING INITIATIVE

Try to imagine the Creator at work. Day after day, God added new dimensions to His creation: light, sky, seas, vegetation, the sun, the moon, stars, fish, birds, and animals. Each was conceived in the mind of God, and when He spoke, He called them into being. As each creative act was completed, God reviewed His work and announced that it was good.

> *It was at this point that God crowned His creation with a breathtaking initiative: "God said, 'Let us make mankind in our image.'" (Gen. 1:26)*

God made you to reflect something of His own nature and glory so that as people look at you, they would see some reflection of God Himself. This is what gives unique dignity and value to every human life. All of the animals were made by God, but none of them were made like God.

## ENJOYING THE GOODNESS OF GOD

Adam enjoyed life in a garden called Eden, which God had planted near the Tigris and Euphrates Rivers (Gen. 2:8–14). While we can't pinpoint its exact location, it was probably somewhere in the area of modern Iraq.

Life in Eden was awesome. It was so different from anything we have experienced that it is difficult for us to grasp. But it is well worth using our imagination to try.

Adam enjoyed the privilege of working in direct partnership with God. His first task was to name the animals as God brought them to him (Gen. 2:19). Giving names may not sound like significant work, but actually this was the first scientific endeavor. Science, at its heart, is about observing, classifying, and describing, and that was the first work God gave Adam to do.

Everything Adam needed was provided in the garden. His work was fulfilling, he was protected from danger, and he enjoyed perfect health. It was heaven on earth.

The greatest joy of life in Eden was the immediate, visible presence of God. God is Spirit, and so He is invisible to us. But in the Garden of Eden, God took on a visible form so that Adam could know Him. We call this a theophany. God came and walked with Adam in the garden (Gen. 3:8).

## A MARRIAGE MADE IN HEAVEN

God saw that it was not good for Adam to be alone, and so the Lord made a woman and brought her to the man

(Gen. 2:18, 22). Imagine Adam's delight when God made the introduction!

God could have created Eve and left the two of them to find each other in the garden. But He didn't do that. God was actively involved in bringing the two of them together. Try to picture God joining their hands and giving His blessing on their shared life together.

The first couple would face their share of problems in the future, but they could never doubt that they had been joined together by God. That is true of every marriage, and that is why marriage is sacred.

*A View from the First Mountain*

---

Pause for a moment to take in this view of the world as God made it. Imagine what it must have been like to live in this perfect environment: sharing the joys of a loving and intimate marriage; growing in knowledge, experience, and skill through creative and fulfilling work; and most of all, cultivating a deep relationship with God, whose visits to the garden brought great delight.

Life as we know it is only a shadow of the mountaintop experience our first parents enjoyed in Eden. God wants you to know what their life was like and how you can recover what has been lost.

It's time to leave the first mountain of the Bible story. We move on reluctantly because the next stop on our journey is a deep valley.

We have made some wonderful discoveries here. God is the Creator of all things. He made everything good. He has created men and women in His own image, giving unique dignity and value to every life.

Some may believe that life is richer when God is at a distance, but the mountaintop experience of life in the Garden of Eden teaches us that life is never richer than when God is near.

*Chapter 2*

---

# **curse**

**IF LIFE WAS SO GOOD** in the Garden of Eden, why is it so different today? The answer to that question lies in the first valley of the Bible story.

When God put Adam in the Garden of Eden, He said, "You are free to eat from any tree in the garden; but you must not eat from the tree of the knowledge of good and evil, for when you eat of it you will certainly die" (Gen. 2:16–17).

Adam and Eve already knew about good. They had never experienced anything else, and God wanted to keep them from the knowledge of evil. In His loving command,

God was saying, "There is a power at work in the wider universe called evil. You don't know anything about it, and I don't want you ever to experience it. I want you to live in freedom from its terrible destructive power. Don't touch evil. It will destroy you."

## WHERE DID EVIL COME FROM?

The Bible never gives us a full explanation of the origin of evil, but it does tell us where it began. Alongside the visible world that we know, God made an invisible creation in heaven and filled it with angels.

One of these angels came to be known as Satan (the name means "adversary"). He became inflated with pride and tried to usurp the position of God (see Isa. 14:12–14). Pride lies at the root of all evil.

The rebellion was unsuccessful and led to Satan being excluded from the presence of God and cast down to the earth. So right from the beginning of human history, there was already an enemy bent on destroying the work of God, and his first aim was to introduce the man and the woman to the knowledge of evil.

## RECRUITING FOR THE REBELLION

Satan came into the Garden of Eden with the aim of recruiting the human race into his rebellion against God. He came in the form of an alluring serpent, presenting himself as a friend, and began to question God's command.

> *"God knows that when you eat of it [the tree] your eyes will be opened, and you will be like God," he said (Gen. 3:5). "Eat from this tree," Satan was essentially saying, "and you will have everything. You've got the knowledge of good, but if you want to be complete, you need the knowledge of evil."*

Adam and Eve decided that this was what they wanted. They broke God's command, and in that act of disobedience, they gained the knowledge of evil. We all have lived with it ever since. The knowledge of evil became a power that was passed on to every person in each generation and in every culture.

The knowledge of evil is the primary problem of the human race. You can't read a newspaper without being reminded that after all the advances of human history we still struggle with evil in all its ugly forms.

The struggle is not just around us, it is also inside us. Why is it that you would do something that made you miserable the last time you did it? There is a power at work in all of us that none of us can fully understand. We are all born to this struggle.

## HOPE IN A CURSE

God will never allow evil to have the last word. He came to the garden and confronted Satan, announcing that his rebel kingdom would not stand. "Cursed are you," God said (Gen. 3:14). When a person or thing is cursed, it is consigned to destruction. So when God cursed the serpent, He was announcing that evil would not stand. Then God spoke about a deliverer who would crush the serpent's head (3:15). When Adam and Eve heard this, they must have been overjoyed.

Then God turned to Adam and again spoke that condemning word: "Cursed . . ." Adam must have felt that he would be caught up in Satan's destruction. But instead of saying to Adam "cursed are you," as the Lord did to the serpent, God said, "Cursed is the ground because of you" (3:17).

God deflected the curse away from Adam so that it fell on the ground and not on him. In this way, God diverted His judgment away from Adam, creating room for a future reconciliation. On the day he sinned, Adam discovered the grace and mercy of God. The curse that should have been on him went to another place. That tells you one of the most important things you need to know about the God of the Bible—He is a God of mercy as well as justice.

## EXCLUDED FROM THE GARDEN

There is no place for evil in the presence of God. Just as Satan's rebellion led to his being cast out of heaven, so our first parents' sin led to their being excluded from the garden where they had known the blessing and presence of God (Gen. 3:23).

Life became a daily struggle in a hostile place. Adam and Eve's perfect marriage was strained, and their work was frustrated as thorns and thistles sprouted from the ground. And when evening came, they must have wondered if God would come and walk with them, but He never did.

Over time, they would notice lines and wrinkles in their skin. They would experience pain and discover that the death God had spoken about was a terrible reality they could not avoid.

God placed cherubim—angels representing His judgment and holiness—at the entrance to the garden, along with "a flaming sword flashing back and forth," barring the way to the Tree of Life (Gen. 3:24). Adam and Eve were alienated from God and left alone in a hostile world. Paradise was lost, and there seemed to be no way back.

*Darkness in the First Valley*

This is the Bible's analysis of the human problem: we have the knowledge of evil, and we have been excluded from the place where God's presence and blessing were known.

The curse is the first valley of the Bible story. The world became a dark place. The rest of the story is about what

God has done to shine His light into our darkness, to deliver us from evil, and to open the way back to paradise. So let's head for the second mountain.

*Chapter 3*

---

# promise

**IMAGINE EVE'S TERROR** and then her joy as she gave birth to the first human baby. Cain seemed to bring fresh hope to the darkened world, but years later that hope was dashed when he killed his brother, Abel (Gen. 4:8). The world's first baby became the world's first murderer. The world's first family was splintered, and in their deep pain, the world's first parents cried out to God for help (4:26).

Evil and violence multiplied as the generations of human history passed. One act of disobedience in the garden led to a tide of violence that swept across the earth:

"The Lord saw how great the wickedness of the human race had become on the earth, and that every inclination of the thoughts of the human heart was only evil all the time" (6:5).

God had not forgotten His promise that evil would not stand, so He intervened, cutting back the human race to a single family through a devastating flood (Gen. 6–7). God was merciful to Noah and his family, who had believed God and acted in obedience to His commands. They were kept safe through the Flood and given the responsibility of making a new start for humanity. But they carried the seeds of sin into the new world with them, and it was not long before the human rebellion against God had regained momentum.

God intervened a second time by confusing human language (Gen. 11). This judgment caused people to divide into language groups that quickly developed their own distinct cultures. And as they spread across the face of the earth, the seeds of future conflict were already sown.

Then God stepped into human history in a new initiative of grace that broke through in the life of a man named Abraham.

## GOD'S GREAT PROMISE OF BLESSING

Abraham neither knew nor worshiped God. He was born around 2000 BC and raised east of the Euphrates River, where he and his family worshiped idols (Josh. 24:2). When people don't know the God who made them, they instinctively put something or someone else in His place. Abraham's idols were his attempt to give meaning and purpose to his life.

One day, God appeared to Abraham (Acts 7:2), like He had appeared to Adam in the garden. Abraham must have wondered why God had chosen to speak with him. The Bible gives us no explanation. All we know is that when the world was in great darkness, God made Himself known to one man, and we should all be deeply thankful for that.

> *God gave Abraham a special promise: "I will make you into a great nation, and I will bless you," He said. "All peoples on earth will be blessed through you." (Gen. 12:2–3)*

Later, God confirmed and expanded His promise. Abraham would have many descendants, and God would give them land from the River Nile to the Euphrates (15:5, 18). These promises must have been perplexing to Abraham because the land God had spoken about was already populated, and Abraham had no children. It seemed impossible, but Abraham believed God's promise (15:6).

## FAITH TESTED TO THE LIMIT

Abraham's faith was tested to the limit. His wife, Sarah, was well past the age for bearing children when God gave the promise of a child, and the idea seemed so ridiculous to her that she laughed when she heard about it (Gen. 18:12).

God was faithful to His promise, and Sarah gave birth to a son. She called him Isaac, which means "laughter" (21:5–6). God brought joy to this elderly couple, and eventually to the whole world, because it was through a descendant of Abraham that God would bless every nation on the face of the earth.

Some years later, God stretched Abraham's faith even further. He told Abraham to take Isaac to Mount Moriah and sacrifice him there as a burnt offering. The thought of a father sacrificing his son is so repulsive to us and to

God that we may easily miss the point of the story. God had promised that His blessing would come to all nations through Abraham's descendants. Now He was showing Abraham the cost at which that blessing would come.

Abraham obeyed God and went to Mount Moriah. He built an altar and placed his son there. Isaac would have been a young man at the time, so forget any artistic impression you may have seen of a young child lying helpless on the altar. Isaac carried the wood on his shoulders (22:6). He was in the prime of life, and if he had wanted to, he could easily have overpowered Abraham, who was over a hundred years old.

God intervened at the critical moment: "Do not lay a hand on the boy," He said. Then Abraham saw a ram caught in a thicket, so he took the ram and sacrificed it as a burnt offering instead of his son (22:12–13).

God had never intended that Abraham should sacrifice Isaac. The story of a father being ready to give up his son and a son being ready to lay down his life shines a powerful light on what it would cost for the promise of God to be fulfilled and His blessing to come for all people (Rom. 8:32).

One day, God would do what Abraham and Isaac could only illustrate. God the Father gave up His Son. God the Son gave Himself for us (Gal. 2:20). The promised Son took our place and was offered as the sacrifice for our sins.

### A View from the Second Mountain

God's promises to Abraham form the second great mountain peak of the Bible story. From this mountain, we can catch a glimpse of what lies ahead. God had promised to bless people from every nation on earth, and He pledged to do it through the line of descendants that would come from Abraham (Gen. 22:17). From this point onward, the action will focus on these people, to whom God's promises were given.

Abraham lived long enough to enjoy Isaac, the promised son. But it would be four hundred years before his descendants would receive the Promised Land. The story of what happened during that time will take us down into the second valley.

## Chapter 4

# pain

**GOD BLESSED ABRAHAM'S** grandson Jacob with a large family, and, in time, his twelve sons became the fathers of the twelve tribes of Israel. God kept His promise to Abraham, and His blessing was on this extended family that would one day become a great nation.

The family was not without its problems. Tensions among the brothers focused on Joseph. God had given him a dream that seemed to indicate Joseph would be given a position of prominence over his brothers. The brothers were not impressed, and they decided that it was time to teach Joseph a lesson in humility.

One day, when they were out in the fields, Joseph's

brothers attacked him. They threw him in a pit and left him there until some traveling traders came by. They sold Joseph to the travelers, who took him to Egypt, and the brothers returned home to tell their father, Jacob, that Joseph had been killed by a wild animal. Jacob was inconsolable in his grief (Gen. 37).

This story takes us down into the second valley, where we discover the suffering of the family God had chosen to bless. Because God promised His blessing to all nations through the line of Abraham's descendants, the hope of the world was tied to the future of this troubled family.

## CRUEL REWARDS FOR INTEGRITY

When the travelers arrived in Egypt, they sold Joseph to Potiphar, a distinguished official in Pharaoh's government (Gen. 39:1). God gave Joseph success in everything he did, and eventually Potiphar put Joseph in charge of his household (39:3–4). But things got complicated when Potiphar's wife tried to seduce him and Joseph ran from the house. Seeking revenge, Potiphar's wife claimed that he had tried to rape her. By the end of the day, Joseph found himself incarcerated alongside the king's prisoners.

It was harsh treatment for a man who had acted with integrity.

God was with Joseph in prison and gave him the ability to accurately predict the future by interpreting dreams. Pharaoh had been troubled by dreams in which he had seen seven fat cows eaten by seven thin cows, and so when he heard about Joseph, he sent for him. Joseph told Pharaoh that God was showing him what the future held. Seven years of abundant harvests would be followed by seven years of famine (41:28–30).

Pharaoh recognized that God had revealed this to Joseph and put him in charge of building reserves of grain that would sustain the population during the coming years of famine. Joseph became the fastest rising star in political history, and next to Pharaoh, he became the most powerful man in Egypt (41:39–40).

## GOD MEANT IT FOR GOOD

Meanwhile back in Canaan, Joseph's father and brothers knew nothing of the coming famine and did nothing to prepare for it. When the famine came, they were desperate. Hearing news that there was grain in Egypt, Joseph's brothers traveled there in the hope of finding food.

They knew nothing of what God had done for Joseph. At first they did not recognize him, and when he eventually revealed his identity to them, they were terrified (Gen. 45:3). But Joseph forgave them. He saw that God had been at work even in the painful experiences of his life. Through an extraordinary chain of cruel events involving the brothers, the slave traders, and Potiphar's wife, God had put Joseph in a position to save the family He had chosen to bless from being wiped out by the famine. "It was to save lives that God sent me ahead of you," he said. "You intended to harm me, but God intended it for good" (Gen. 45:5; 50:20).

## THE FIRST HOLOCAUST

The family God had chosen to bless settled in Egypt. There were seventy-five of them when they arrived (Acts 7:14), and in the years that followed, the family prospered. But things changed quickly when a new ruler came to power in Egypt (Ex. 1:8). He was troubled by the rapid growth of the Israelites, so he launched a fierce persecution against them, forcing them to work in fields and on building sites for long hours in dreadful conditions (Ex. 1:9, 14).

God's people continued to thrive even under oppression, and so Pharaoh introduced his final solution: state-sponsored infanticide. He ordered that every newborn male child should be drowned in the River Nile (Ex. 1:22). Pharaoh's racial prejudice blinded him to the unique dignity and value of every human life. It was the first holocaust.

The new pharaoh knew nothing about Joseph and nothing about the God of the Bible who had saved His nation from disaster in the famine. Where God is not known, human life is not valued; and where human life is not valued, evil will soon be unleashed.

God had protected His people from the famine in Egypt, but it was never His purpose that they should stay there. And it was through this fierce and prolonged persecution that the Hebrews who had once been comfortably settled in Egypt began to cry out to God for rescue.

After four hundred years in which there had been no significant progress in God's plan to bring blessing to the human race, God was about to step into the course of history again and bring His people into the land He had promised.

*A View from the Second Valley*

In the second valley, we are confronted with the reality of evil and the mystery of suffering. Why did God allow the people He had blessed to experience so much pain? God has not chosen to answer that question fully. But the second valley of the Bible story shows us that even our most painful suffering will find its place in the ultimate purpose of God.

*Chapter 5*

---

# covenant

**FIVE HUNDRED YEARS** after God appeared to Abraham, his descendants numbered around two million people. They were oppressed in Egypt and their outlook seemed bleak.

But God had not forgotten His people or His promise to give them their own land. After four hundred years of silence, the God who appeared to Abraham, Isaac, and Jacob intercepted the life of a man called Moses.

God's hand had been on Moses from his earliest days. Moses' mother hid him in a basket on the banks of the River Nile to save him from the slaughter of Hebrew babies; Pharaoh's daughter found him and raised him as a prince in the palace, but later Moses fled from Egypt to begin an anonymous life in the desert.

## THE SELF-SUSTAINING FIRE

That was where God stepped in. Moses saw a fire resting on a bush, but it did not burn the bush on which it rested. The fire was self-sustaining. All other fires go out when they have exhausted the available fuel. A candle burns only until the wax is gone, and then the flame goes out. But this flame was unlike any other. It sustained its own life. God is self-sustaining. He does not depend on anyone or anything.

As Moses drew closer, God spoke to him out of the fire: "I am the God of your father, the God of Abraham, the God of Isaac and the God of Jacob" (Ex. 3:6). Then God revealed the name by which He wanted to be known: "I AM WHO I AM" (3:14).

Then God commissioned Moses to bring His people out of Egypt (3:10). Moses confronted Pharaoh with God's command: "Let my people go" (5:1). But Pharaoh refused. But after a series of plagues had devastated his kingdom, Pharaoh finally agreed to God's demand.

## REFLECTING THE CHARACTER OF GOD

Two months later, God's people set up camp at Mount Sinai. They remained there for ten months, and God used that time to turn a confused crowd into a disciplined nation.

The first priority for the people was to understand their unique calling. They were God's people, the heirs of God's promises to Abraham. God confirmed His commitment to them in a covenant: "I will walk among you and be your God, and you will be my people" (Lev. 26:12).

Then God gave His people the Ten Commandments. This is not an arbitrary list of rules or a culturally conditioned set of values. These commandments are a direct reflection of the character of God. When God says, "You shall have no other gods before me," it is because He is the only God. When God says, "You shall not commit adultery," it is because He is faithful. And when He says, "You shall not covet," it is because God is at peace in Himself, and He calls His people to be like Him (Ex. 20:3, 14, 17).

Keeping the Law does not make us God's people, but being God's people means that we are called to reflect His character by living according to His Law.

## PLUNGED INTO CRISIS

A few weeks later, God's people were plunged into crisis. While Moses was away from the people, they made an idol and indulged in all kinds of depravity (Ex. 32:5–6). Their behavior was a contradiction rather than a reflection of God's character.

God told His people that He would give them the land of Canaan, but because of their sin, they would not enjoy the gift of His presence (Ex. 33:3). When the people heard this, they were brokenhearted. They understood that the gifts of freedom and prosperity would mean little without the presence and blessing of God, and they longed for their relationship with God to be restored.

## A PLACE TO MEET WITH GOD

God gave Moses detailed instructions for a mobile worship center called the tabernacle. At the center of this tent-like structure was the Most Holy Place. The ark of the covenant was placed there. It was a wooden chest covered by a lid with statues of cherubim, the angelic figures that had guarded the entrance to the Garden of Eden.

This was where God would meet with a representative of His people called the high priest (Ex. 25:22). When the high priest went into the Most Holy Place and sprinkled the blood of a sacrificed animal between the cherubim, a cloud representing God's immediate presence filled the tabernacle.

God was showing how His presence would return to His people. The cherubim were a visual reminder that sin always brings death. But the blood of the sacrificed animal spoke of God's readiness to accept a substitute.

## MOVING FORWARD WITH GOD

God's people moved forward from Sinai and headed for Canaan. God's presence was with them, and He was ready to give them the land He had promised to Abraham. But the land was already occupied, and God's people lacked the courage to fight. Without faith, they could not enjoy the fulfillment of God's promise, so they wandered in the desert for forty years until a new generation was ready to step forward in obedience.

God's people entered the Promised Land under the

leadership of Moses' successor, Joshua. In this one event, God accomplished two purposes: fulfilling His covenant promise and bringing judgment.

God had told Abraham that there would be a long delay before his descendants would inherit the Promised Land, because "the sin of the Amorites has not yet reached its full measure" (Gen. 15:16). Five hundred years later it had. God had seen their persistent atrocities, and so He brought about their downfall.

## A View from the Third Mountain

When the land was settled, Joshua called the people to renew their covenant with God. In less than fifty years, God had brought His people from slavery in Egypt to prosperity in Canaan. "We too will serve the LORD," they said (Josh. 24:18).

It was a great moment. But it would not be long before God's people found their way into another dark valley.

*Chapter 6*

---

# chaos

**IT TAKES ONLY ONE** generation to change a culture, and amazingly, after all God had done, that was all it took for His people to forget Him altogether. After Joshua and his generation had died, "another generation grew up who knew neither the LORD nor what he had done for Israel" (Judg. 2:10). This was the beginning of a dark time for God's people that was to last about three hundred years (ca. 1300–1000 BC).

God had given His people everything they needed for the new nation to thrive. Each of the twelve tribes had its own leadership, and each was committed to the defense of the others. They lived under the same laws designed to foster God-centered living, and their unity was strengthened by the regular festivals of thanksgiving that they shared.

But within a generation, all this had gone. Participation in the festivals declined, alternative venues were organized, and soon the sense of national unity was lost. The commitment of the tribes to mutual defense diminished, and instead of living together under the Law of God, "everyone did as they saw fit" (Judg. 17:6; 21:25). The result, of course, was chaos.

## GOING ROUND IN CIRCLES

The book of Judges records a cycle of events that recurred many times over a period of about three hundred years. It began when God's people turned to idols (Judg. 2:11–12). God had called His people to live in a way that reflected His character. So when they wanted to do what was right in their own eyes, they developed their own gods who would approve what they wanted to do.

This was a direct violation of the first commandment, so God gave them into the hands of their enemies, who invaded the land and plundered them (2:14).

Then the people would cry out to God for help, and God would raise up a leader (called a judge) to deliver them (2:16). God's Spirit came on these military leaders, giving them success in battle. They would restore security, and typically there would be peace throughout the judge's lifetime. But soon after the judge died, the people would return to idols, and the whole cycle would begin again (2:18–19).

## GIFTS WITHOUT CHARACTER

The best known and certainly the most colorful of all the judges was Samson. God gave him an unusual gift of physical strength, which enabled him to achieve remarkable victories for God's people.

Samson was a larger-than-life hero who inspired hope when everything else seemed lost. In a country overrun by enemies, here was one man who could put up a fight for the liberation of his people with awesome results. He was able to take out one thousand Philistines in hand-to-hand combat, armed with only the jawbone of a dead donkey (Judg. 15:15).

The problem was that his physical strength was not

matched by moral character. His marriage and personal life were chaotic, and at times he behaved like a juvenile delinquent! Samson's gift outweighed his character, and his story leaves the reader thinking, *Surely God must have a better deliverer for His people to follow than this!*

## LOOKING FOR LEADERS

In the absence of clear leadership and an agreed moral foundation, life in Canaan became increasingly chaotic. Discontent was rising among God's people, and they started to look around them for a new kind of leadership.

The obvious weakness was that the judges lacked continuity. Other nations had kings with standing armies, and when a king died, his successor was crowned immediately.

God had not appointed a king among His people for the simple reason that God Himself was their King. But relying on God meant living by faith, and the people felt that they would rather have a flesh and blood person to lead them.

God warned the people about the demands future kings would make, but their minds were made up. They wanted a king (1 Sam. 8:8–20). So God gave them what they asked for, and Samuel anointed Saul as the first king of Israel.

## A BIG DISAPPOINTMENT

Saul had the style and stature of a monarch, but he turned out to be a big disappointment. His early victories went to his head, and he felt that he could be selective in his obedience to God's commands. He was convinced that as long as he was offering sacrifices to God all would be well. He had not understood that religious ritual is empty if unaccompanied by obedience to God (1 Sam. 15:22).

Samuel the prophet had the unenviable task of confronting Saul. "You have rejected the word of the LORD," he said, "and the LORD has rejected you as king over Israel" (15:26).

Saul could have accepted God's discipline and begun a new chapter of obedience. But he didn't. He became obsessed with a relentless pursuit of David, whom God had chosen as the next king of Israel, and he spent his later years trying to destroy the future.

In the end, Saul took his own life on the field of battle (31:4). It was a sad end to a tragic life and brought closure at last to the long dark valley of chaos that God's people had experienced.

*A View from the Third Valley*

The third valley teaches us that choices matter. When a nation turns from God's Law, the fabric of society will soon unravel. Impressive leaders who lack integrity will always bring disappointment in the end. Poor choices always lead to painful consequences.

But there is also hope in this chaotic valley. God never abandoned His people. Even when they made irreversible choices, such as appointing a king, God remained faithful to His promise and continued to work out His purpose.

God redeems bad decisions, and He advances His purpose for our lives even through circumstances that should never have been. No choice, however poor, can put you beyond the grace of God. That grace was about to break through to God's people again through a new king, whose name was David.

Chapter 7

_____

# kingdom

**DAVID BEGAN HIS LIFE** in obscurity as a shepherd in Bethlehem, the youngest of eight brothers. But God was with him, and after he defeated Goliath, the champion of Israel's enemy, everybody knew who David was. God's people had a hero.

Of course, that wasn't the way King Saul saw it! When the ancient equivalent of cheerleaders started singing, "Saul has slain his thousands, and David his tens of thousands" (1 Sam. 18:7), it nearly drove Saul crazy. David had to flee for his life, but God's hand was on him. And when Saul died, David was crowned as king.

David's first move was to march on Jerusalem. Although

God's people had been in the land for over three hundred years, they had not occupied that great city. David captured Jerusalem and established his palace and center of government there (2 Sam. 5).

## RAIDERS OF THE LOST ARK

Then David brought the ark of the covenant to Jerusalem (2 Sam. 6). It was a day of great celebration. When God's people were in the desert, God's visible presence had come down to the ark. But during the reign of King Saul, the ark had been placed in storage and completely forgotten. That tells you something about the spiritual life of the nation at the time.

David wanted the symbol of the presence of God to be at the center of national life, so he brought the ark to Jerusalem. He was living in a magnificent palace, and it seemed inappropriate to him that the ark, where God made Himself at home, should be covered by canvas.

The king wanted to build a temple to house the ark, but God had other plans, which He announced to David through the prophet Nathan. David wanted to do something impressive for God, but God was preparing to do something spectacular for David—and for the whole human race.

## A SPECTACULAR PROMISE

"I will raise up your offspring to succeed you . . . and I will establish his kingdom," God said. "He is the one who will build a house for my Name, and I will establish the throne of his kingdom forever. I will be his father, and he will be my son" (2 Sam. 7:12–14).

David was overwhelmed by the weight and glory of these promises. It was easy to understand that his son would build a temple, but how could a son of David be described as God's son? And how could any king's reign last forever? God was promising to do something beyond David's wildest imagination.

The whole story is about how God's blessing would come to all people. God had already promised that His blessing would come through a descendant of Abraham. Now, a thousand years later, God was making it clear that it would come through a king descended from the line of David. This promise narrows the search for the person who would be instrumental in fulfilling the promises of God.

## UNPARALLELED BLESSING

David became king about a thousand years before the birth of Christ, and he reigned for forty years (2 Sam. 5:4). During that time, God's people enjoyed unparalleled blessing. Under David's strong leadership, Israel's enemies were subdued, and her borders were secured. With strong defense, a thriving economy, and stable leadership, God's people had never had it so good.

## SOLOMON'S TEMPLE

After David died, God's blessing continued through the reign of his son Solomon, who set about fulfilling his father's plans for a temple in Jerusalem. It was a massive construction project involving 30,000 men felling timber in Lebanon, 80,000 stonecutters, 70,000 carriers, and 3,300 foremen working in the quarries (1 Kings 5:13–16).

Solomon paid particular attention to the inner area of the temple. In the old tabernacle, the Most Holy Place had been screened off by a curtain, but in the new temple, it was an unlit room about thirty feet square and thirty feet high. It was a perfect cube (6:20).

Solomon placed two massive sculptures of angelic figures, called cherubim, in the Most Holy Place (6:23–28). The wingspan of these cherubim covered the entire room, indicating the separation of man from God.

When the building was complete, God's people gathered for a service of dedication. The priests brought the ark of the covenant into the temple and put it in the Most Holy Place, beneath the wings of the cherubim (8:6).

When the priests withdrew, a remarkable thing happened. The cloud of God's glorious presence filled the temple (8:10–11). The last time God had shown the glory of His presence in a visible way like this was in the desert more than four hundred years earlier. Now the same God whose glory had come down and rested on the ark had come to Solomon's temple. Solomon's first response was to worship. God's presence was with His people. At last there was a place on earth where God's presence could be known (8:29).

*A View from the Fourth Mountain*

Solomon reigned for forty years. He became famous for his wisdom, and royal visitors came from all over the world to admire his achievements. He accumulated massive wealth, and during his reign, Israel became the envy of the world. God's people were on the mountaintop in the days of David and Solomon.

Sadly, in his latter years, Solomon, who had been known for his unusual wisdom, made some foolish mistakes. With all his attention focused on Jerusalem in the south, he alienated people in the north, planting the seeds of future division.

Solomon's international celebrity status was the root of his downfall. He disobeyed the Lord by marrying many women who worshiped other gods (1 Kings 11:1). They persuaded him to build places of worship for their gods, and by the end of his reign, idolatry had taken root among God's people. It was the beginning of another long dark valley.

*Chapter 8*

---

# conflict

**AFTER THE DEATH OF** Solomon, tensions increased between the ten tribes in the north and the two tribes in the south, where power and wealth were concentrated around Jerusalem.

Solomon's son Rehoboam made matters worse. He regarded the northern tribes as rebels and set about subduing them with a program of forced labor. The northern tribes responded by declaring their independence and crowning Jeroboam, their rebel leader, as king.

This sad division among God's people was very significant. God had promised to bless people from every nation through a king from the line of David. When the northern tribes crowned their own king, they were separating themselves from that promise and from the blessing of God.

## RELIGION, POLITICS, AND VIOLENCE

Jeroboam was a shrewd leader. He saw that if faithful people from the north kept visiting Jerusalem to worship the Lord in the temple, they would be reminded of God's promise and might renew their allegiance to the line of David. So he crafted two golden calves and established his own center of worship in the north (1 Kings 12:28).

Jeroboam had no interest in obeying the Lord. He was using religion merely to strengthen the identity of his people. And when that is the aim, any religion will do.

In the south, where the royal line of David continued, a king typically transferred power to his son as he approached death. But in the north, there was no established royal house and no recognized line of succession. So political intrigue and violence abounded, and most of the kings came to power by murdering their predecessors.

## PERSECUTING GOD'S PEOPLE

Ahab was the most notorious of the northern kings. His wife, Jezebel, led a furious persecution in which the prophets of God were hunted and killed. In half a century, Israel had gone from a people united in worshiping the Lord to a nation confused and divided. Fifty years after the cloud of God's presence had filled Solomon's temple, the knowledge of God was all but lost, even among His own people.

The social results of turning from God and His laws were disastrous. The prophet Amos described conditions in the northern kingdom in these words: "They sell the innocent for silver, and the needy for a pair of sandals. They trample on the heads of the poor as on the dust of the ground and deny justice to the oppressed. Father and son use the same girl and so profane my holy name" (Amos 2:6–7).

The sad story of the northern kingdom continued for about two hundred years (920–722 BC). There were nineteen kings altogether, and every one of them "did evil in the eyes of the LORD" (see 2 Kings 15:9).

Eventually, God allowed enemies to overrun the northern kingdom. The king of Assyria deported the entire population in 722 BC, dispersing them across the breadth of his kingdom. Later, he repopulated the area with immigrants, who became known as the Samaritans.

## THE STORY IN THE SOUTH

The two tribes in the south, often referred to as Judah, benefited from better leadership than their brothers and sisters in the north. Asa, Jehoshaphat, Joash, Amaziah, Uzziah, and Jotham were all commended by God. But none of them eliminated the places of worship to other gods that had been erected in the days of Solomon. These centers of idolatry continued to be an offense to God.

Things took a turn for the worse in Judah when Manasseh came to power shortly after the northern tribes were scattered. Manasseh reigned for fifty-five years, and he led God's people into more evil than the nations God had driven out of the land (2 Kings 21:1, 9).

Manasseh promoted the worship of Molek, which included an evil rite in which children were sacrificed in a fire. He "consulted mediums and spiritists," and in an ultimate act of defiance toward God, he built altars to pagan gods in the temple of the Lord (2 Kings 21:4–6).

God had called His people to be lights in the world, but Manasseh led them into deep darkness.

## CHANGING LAWS AND CHANGING HEARTS

Some years later Manasseh's grandson Josiah began to seek after the Lord. Stirred by the rediscovery of a manuscript of God's Law that had been lost in the temple, Josiah led a national campaign of reformation. He toured the country and personally supervised the destruction of all the altars to idols in the land (2 Kings 23). Some of these had been built in the time of Solomon and had been standing for three hundred years.

Josiah's reform was the greatest onslaught against pagan practices in the history of Israel. He eliminated idolatry. But changing laws is not the same as changing hearts, and soon after the death of Josiah, the altars to idols were rebuilt, and the patterns of sin associated with them resumed.

*A View from the Fourth Valley*

The tragic story of the divided kingdom teaches us that when a nation turns away from God, dark powers of evil are unleashed. God's people chose to worship gods of their own making. They turned from the light and eventually were devoured by darkness.

But God never abandoned His people. He kept speaking to them through the prophets, even when they turned to other gods. Isaiah, Jeremiah, Hosea, Joel, Amos, Obadiah, Micah, Nahum, and Habakkuk all called God's people to repentance during these dark years of the divided kingdom. But God's people were not listening to God's Word.

So, after repeated warnings, the time for God's judgment on His own people finally came. The Babylonian army laid siege to Jerusalem and remained there for nearly two years, until the city fell in 586 BC. The suffering of God's people was indescribable. Many lost their lives, and most of those who survived were taken to resettlement camps in Babylon.

The city of Jerusalem became a smoldering ruin. The

temple where God had chosen to meet with His people was totally destroyed. The great kingdom that had been the envy of the world in the time of David and Solomon was reduced to a small community of war prisoners in Babylon. But even in this darkest hour, God had not forgotten His people or His promise.

*Chapter 9*

---

# restoration

**GOD'S PEOPLE WERE** brokenhearted. Their homes had been destroyed, and they had been taken by force to a remote backwater of Babylon called the Kebar River.

God's people sat by the rivers of Babylon and wept. Their great nation had been reduced to a small community of survivors, and Canaan was a desolate wasteland. They thought about the ruined city of Jerusalem and asked, "How can we sing the songs of the LORD while in a foreign land?" (Ps. 137:4).

## HOPE IN THE VALLEY

God spoke to His discouraged people through the prophet Ezekiel. He was given a vision in which he saw a flying platform carrying the throne of God. It hovered over the temple in Jerusalem but then moved away to the east. The significance was obvious. God had abandoned Jerusalem, but He had not abandoned His people or His promises. His plan to bring blessing to the world now focused on this group of exiles who were living seven hundred miles east of Jerusalem. Far from being in a backwater, these people were right in the center of the will of God.

Later, in another vision, Ezekiel saw a valley of dry bones. It was a picture of desolation and death that seemed to be without hope. But as Ezekiel watched, he saw the bones coming together, being covered with flesh, muscle, and skin, and then rising to life like an army. It was a picture of what God would do for His people. Out of the devastation, He would bring new life.

## THE SWEET SEDUCTION OF SUCCESS

Some of God's people prospered in Babylon. King Nebuchadnezzar placed Daniel and other highly gifted young people on an educational fast track that prepared them for glittering careers. The king gave these young students Babylonian names, arranged for their education in Babylonian literature, and gave them a taste of the high life by offering food from the menu served at his own table.

A thousand years earlier, Pharaoh had persecuted God's people and made them slaves. Nebuchadnezzar followed a different plan. Instead of persecution, he offered prosperity. His aim was to dazzle God's people with the opportunities of life in Babylon until they were so caught up in the pursuit of success that they would forget about their distinctive calling as the people of God.

It worked with some of God's people, but others, like Daniel, determined that however successful they became, they would never forget that they belonged to the Lord and that their highest calling was to honor Him.

## CREATING A NEW COMMUNITY

Seventy years after God's people were taken into exile, Babylon fell to the rising empire of the Medes and the Persians. The new king, Cyrus, decreed that any Jewish exiles who wished to return to Jerusalem were free to do so.

A group of about fifty thousand people caught the vision of creating a new community in the city of God and returned under the leadership of Zerubbabel (Ezra 2:64–67). After rebuilding their homes, they built an altar and began offering sacrifices as God had commanded Moses. Then they rebuilt the temple. It was a wonderful achievement that marked a new beginning for the people of God.

*A View from the Fifth Mountain*

God's people were full of enthusiasm, but they had little understanding of God's Law. When a priest by the name of Ezra came to visit, he was appalled at the spiritual condition of the people and set about the task of shaping the community by teaching God's Word (Ezra 7:6).

Sometime later, God raised up another leader named Nehemiah. He saw that although the temple had been completed, nothing had been done about the walls. The great city of God had no defenses and had precious little infrastructure. God put it into Nehemiah's heart to do something about these things (Neh. 2:1–18).

When the walls were rebuilt, the people gathered in the public square to worship God. They called on Ezra to bring out the Book of the Law. Ezra must have had great joy in teaching the Word of God to this community of people who were committing themselves to a new life of faith and obedience.

Jerusalem was filled with the sound of music and singing. God's people were back in God's city, and they rejoiced because God had given them great joy (Neh. 12:43).

## SOMETHING MISSING

But something was missing. For anyone who had seen the grandeur of Solomon's temple, the new one was a big disappointment. When the foundations were poured, younger people cheered, but older people who remembered the old temple wept (Ezra 3:12–13). The new building seemed like a poor shadow of the great temple that had once attracted the attention of the world.

The small community of returning exiles simply did not have the resources for a building on the scale of Solomon's temple, and God sent the prophets Haggai and Zechariah to tell them not to "despise the day of small things" (Zech. 4:10; see also Hag. 2:3).

But there was one overarching problem. The Most Holy Place had once housed the ark of the covenant where God's presence had come down. The ark was the meeting place of God and man. But the ark had been destroyed, and it has never been recovered. So the Most Holy Place that had once housed the symbol of God's presence became a conspicuously empty room.

When Solomon's temple was dedicated nearly five hundred years before, the cloud of God's visible presence filled the building. But nothing like this ever happened in the second temple. God's people sang songs of praise. They offered prayers, gifts, and sacrifices, but they were left longing for the presence of God and the fulfillment of His promises.

That continued through another long, dark valley. For four hundred years, God remained silent. Then one day, God spoke to an elderly priest named Zechariah as he was doing his work in the temple. He would have a son and name him John. John's great task would be to prepare

God's people for the coming of the Lord. At last, the time had come. God was about to fulfill His promises to Abraham and to David in the most extraordinary way.

# PART TWO

# Trusting Christ

## the Son

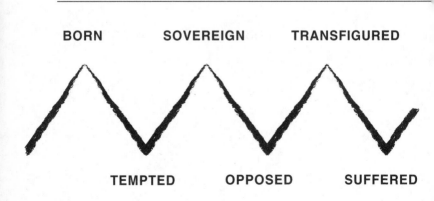

BORN    SOVEREIGN    TRANSFIGURED

TEMPTED    OPPOSED    SUFFERED

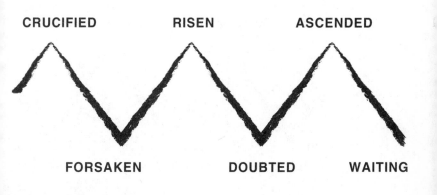

CRUCIFIED        RISEN        ASCENDED

FORSAKEN        DOUBTED        WAITING

**THE OLD TESTAMENT** story set the stage for God's greatest intervention in human history. God had given many clues about the identity of a promised person, often referred to as the Messiah or Christ, who would bring God's blessing to His people and to the nations.

He would be a descendant of Abraham, in the line of David. He would fulfill the role of a prophet (one who speaks the word of God), a priest (one who offers a sacrifice), and a king (one who rules and protects the people). But He would clearly be more than any other prophet, priest, or king had been or ever could be. His kingdom would last forever, and while He would be a son of David, God had said, "I will be his father, and he will be my son" (2 Sam. 7:14).

Whoever this person turned out to be, His entrance into the world would be the greatest event in the entire history of the human race. Everything God had promised to do would be fulfilled by Him.

It is of great significance then that Jesus Christ is introduced in the New Testament as "the son of David, the son of Abraham" (Matt. 1:1). The New Testament continues the story of the Old and tells us how God has accomplished everything He promised to do through Jesus Christ.

*Chapter 10*

---

# born

**THE BIRTH OF JESUS CHRIST** was the first evidence that He is unlike any other person who has ever lived.

This is how it came about: Mary was a young woman preparing for marriage to a man named Joseph. God spoke to her, like He had spoken to Abraham, Moses, and the prophets in the past, only this time He spoke through the angel Gabriel:

> *"Do not be afraid, Mary; you have found favor with God. You will conceive and give birth to a son, and you are to call him Jesus." (Luke 1:30–31)*

Since Mary was a virgin, she could not see how she could possibly have a child. "How will this be . . . ?" she asked (1:34). The angel's answer takes us to the heart of the greatest and most wonderful mystery in the Bible.

> *"The Holy Spirit will come on you, and the power of the Most High will overshadow you. So the holy one to be born will be called the Son of God." (1:35)*

Mary's child was born as the result of a direct initiative of God. Joseph made no contribution whatsoever. He was an outsider, a passive observer to the whole miraculous event. This is important because the Bible contains other stories of miraculous births. Abraham and Sarah had longed for a child, and Isaac's birth was a miracle because they were both well past the age of conceiving children. Isaac was born through a special intervention from God, but his birth still came through the union of a father and a mother.

But Mary was a virgin. The life in her womb came to be there through a creative miracle of God. God did not wait for a deliverer to arise *from* the human race. He came *to* the human race. God became a man, taking flesh from Mary.

## GOD'S INCREDIBLE JOURNEY

Your life began at the moment you were conceived in your mother's womb. Before that moment, you did not exist, and without that, you would not have been! But with Jesus, it is different. His life did not begin in Mary's womb. Before He was born, He shared the life of God in heaven (John 1:1).

The angel announced to Mary that her child would be "the Son of the Most High" and "the Son of God" (Luke 1:32, 35). In a separate appearance to Joseph, He was announced as "Immanuel (which means 'God with us')" (Matt. 1:23). God took on human flesh and came to us, entering human history as a baby.

We will never be able to understand how God could become a man, but the central claim of the New Testament is that He did. This miracle is an unfathomable mystery, but it makes sense of everything else that the Bible tells us about Jesus. If God became a man in Jesus, then His claims, His miracles, and His resurrection should bring no surprise. Everything else in the New Testament revolves around this one miracle.

Being fully God and fully man, Jesus Christ is uniquely

qualified to do everything necessary to reconcile sinners to God. Only God can reconcile us to Himself, and He did it by becoming man in order to bear our sins.

Jesus is the prophet who revealed all that we need to know about God. Jesus is the priest who offered Himself as the sacrifice for our sins. Jesus is the king who will lead His people into the promised blessing of God.

## HE IS HOLY

Jesus Christ was like us in every respect except one. He is holy. This means that He did not at any time commit a single sin. But it means more than that. He was holy in His thoughts, in His intentions, and in His character. His nature was holy. He was not drawn to sin, and He had no inner propensity to sin. There has never been anybody else in human history about whom this could be said.

The holiness of Jesus flows from the fact that He is God. The angel said to Mary, "The holy one to be born will be called the Son of God" (Luke 1:35). Jesus Christ is truly God. Therefore, He is holy.

Jesus was also a man. But it is important to remember that being human is not the same as being sinful. Adam and Eve were holy human beings in the Garden of Eden. After their fall, human nature became so bound up with sin that it is difficult for us to imagine a human being who is not subject to sin and death.

But Jesus is the pioneer of a new humanity, and His holiness opens up a whole new world of hope for us: it is possible for a man or a woman to live for the glory of God and to triumph over sin, death, and hell.

*A View from the First Mountain*

The birth of the Lord Jesus Christ is the first great mountaintop of His life and ministry. Angels filled the skies when He was born, singing, "Glory to God in the highest heaven, and on earth peace to men on whom his favor rests" (Luke 2:14).

Jewish shepherds came to see Him in the manger. And later, wise men came from the east with gifts for the newborn king. Jew and Gentile, rich and poor came to worship Jesus.

Dark and evil forces were also stirred up. King Herod was so troubled by talk of a new king that he ordered the slaughter of all the infant boys in the vicinity of Bethlehem, where Jesus had been born.

God had warned Joseph about this in a dream, and he had already moved the family to safety in Egypt. But it was the beginning of a conflict that would resume thirty years later in the desert.

*Chapter 11*

# tempted

**THE BIRTH OF THE LORD** Jesus Christ must have set alarm bells ringing in hell. The presence of light spells the end for darkness, and God's immediate presence on earth as a man would mean the destruction of evil—unless Satan could find a way to destroy Jesus.

His first attempt came through the rage of King Herod, whose murder of innocent children in the region of Bethlehem was an intolerable crime. But when that dark deed failed, Satan was forced out into the open in a direct confrontation with Jesus.

## BAPTIZED AND FILLED WITH THE SPIRIT

Jesus was about thirty years of age when He began His public ministry. He was baptized in the River Jordan, identifying Himself fully with men and women who were seeking to live for the glory of God. The Holy Spirit descended on Jesus, and an audible voice from heaven said, "This is my Son, whom I love; with him I am well pleased" (Matt. 3:17).

Filled with the Holy Spirit, Jesus went into the desert, where He endured a period of intense temptation that lasted forty days. It is significant that the Spirit led Jesus into the desert (Luke 4:1). Christ was stalking the enemy. He had come into the world to destroy Satan's work, and the first step in His public ministry was to confront our enemy and triumph where Adam had failed.

## CONFUSION, PRESUMPTION, AND AMBITION

Satan appears to have a limited number of strategies. That much is evident from the parallels between his successful tempting of Adam and Eve, and his total failure to compromise the integrity of the Lord Jesus Christ.

Satan's first strategy in both cases was an attempt to

create confusion. In the Garden of Eden, he asked Eve, "Did God really say, 'You must not eat from any tree in the garden'?" (Gen. 3:1). In the desert, the enemy tried to create confusion about Jesus' identity. "If you are the Son of God," he said, "tell these stones to become bread" (Matt. 4:3).

His second strategy in the garden was an attempt to promote presumption. Satan tried to convince Eve that she could disobey the command of God without consequence. "You will not certainly die," he said (Gen. 3:4). He used the same line of argument against Jesus when he led Him to the highest point of the temple and said, "If you are the Son of God . . . throw yourself down" (Matt. 4:6).

The third strategy centered on ambition. Satan promised Eve that asserting her independence would put her in a position of equality with God. "You will be like God," he said (Gen. 3:5). Having succeeded with this strategy once, the enemy tried the same approach against Jesus: "I will give you all [the] authority and splendor [of the kingdoms of the world] . . . if you worship me" (Luke 4:5–7).

Satan launched everything he had in his assault against the Lord Jesus Christ, but he could not break Him. After he had exhausted every strategy he knew, he was left with no alternative but to retreat.

## FACING THE FULL FORCE OF THE ENEMY

Jesus faced the full power of the enemy. Although He was sinless, the temptation he faced was greater than we will ever know.

Imagine three airmen flying jets over enemy territory during a war. They are shot down, captured, and then taken by the enemy for interrogation. One by one, they are brought into a darkened room.

The first airman gives his name, rank, and serial number. His captors ask him for the positions of his forces. He knows that he must not give this information, but he also knows that the enemy is cruel and eventually will break him. So why go through all that? He tells them what he knows.

The second airman is brought in. He also gives his name, rank, and serial number, and they begin to pump him for information. He is determined not to give in. So the cruelty begins. Eventually, it overwhelms him. He breaks and tells them what he knows.

Then the third airman comes in and gives his name, rank, and serial number. "You will not break me," he says.

"Oh yes, we will. We have broken every man who has ever come into this room. It is only a matter of time; you'll see."

The cruelty begins, but he does not break. So it is intensified, and still he does not break. It is intensified once more, until it feels unbearable, but still he does not break.

Finally, there comes a point when they have tried everything they know. "It's no use," they say. "He is not like any other person we've had in this room. We can't break him."

Which of these airmen faced the full force of the enemy?

The only one to know the full force of the enemy's assault is the one who did not break. So don't ever think that Christ's temptations were less than yours. Only Christ knows the full power of temptation, because only Christ has withstood the full force of the enemy's assault.

*A View from the First Valley*

When the Son of God took on our human flesh, He became another Adam. Jesus confronted our enemy and triumphed where Adam had failed. Adam's failure brought the tragic consequence of death to the entire human race. But Jesus' triumph brings everlasting life for all who are joined to Him by faith.

The forty-day confrontation with Satan in the desert was the first dark valley through which our Lord Jesus Christ had to go. Having faced and exhausted the full force of the enemy's assault, He was ready to begin a public ministry in which people would see the blessings of life in the kingdom of God.

## Chapter 12

# sovereign

**JESUS LAUNCHED HIS PUBLIC** ministry by announcing His mission and purpose. He was attending a Sabbath service at the synagogue in His hometown of Nazareth, and as He stood up to read an attendant gave Him a scroll of the prophet Isaiah. Opening the scroll, Jesus read these words:

> *"The Spirit of the Lord is upon me,*
> *because he has anointed me*
> *to proclaim good news to the poor.*
> *He has sent me to proclaim liberty to the captives*
> *and recovering of sight to the blind,*

> *to set at liberty those who are oppressed,*
> *to proclaim the year of the Lord's favor."*
> *(Luke 4:18–19)*

The words were familiar to the audience. They had been read in services of worship for more than seven hundred years. But God's people were still waiting for the hope that they promised.

## A DRAMATIC ANNOUNCEMENT

When Jesus had finished reading, He rolled up the scroll, handed it back to the attendant, and sat down, as rabbis always did when they taught. The people were well used to the routine of the reading and the sermon, but nobody was prepared for the drama of Jesus' announcement: "Today," He said, "this scripture is fulfilled in your hearing" (Luke 4:21).

Others had explained what the Messiah would do. Jesus announced that the Messiah had come.

## THE MISSION OF JESUS

Jesus announced Himself as the promised deliverer. Through His unique ministry, prisoners would be released, the eyes of the blind would be opened, and people who were oppressed would find freedom.

When Jesus said that He had come to proclaim the year of the Lord's favor, He was referring to a year of celebration that God had instituted in the Old Testament called the Jubilee (Lev. 25).

God's plan was that every fifty years, unpaid debts would be forgiven, slaves would be released, and land that had been sold in times of hardship would be returned to the original owners. The Jubilee offered a new beginning for all of God's people, as old debts were forgiven and lost inheritances were restored.

The Jubilee laws were a wonderful blessing for the poor, but a costly obligation for the rich. That is why the Jubilee never happened in the entire history of the Old Testament. Those who had the power to call the Jubilee never had the will to do so. It was just too costly.

Jesus came to announce God's Jubilee, and that is good news for the poor. Christ is willing to forgive our old debts to God and to restore our lost inheritance. He is able to release those who are imprisoned by sin and oppressed by Satan. The blessing that God had promised for all people through someone in the line of Abraham and David has come in Jesus Christ.

## HEALING THE SICK

Over the next three years Jesus gave stunning evidence of His ability to deliver on these remarkable promises. A blind man received his sight (John 9), a deaf man received the gift of hearing (Mark 7), and a man who had been crippled for thirty-eight years walked (John 5)—to name only a few. In all these miracles, Jesus was moved by compassion. He reached into the suffering of broken lives, bringing healing and hope.

Jesus even healed people suffering from leprosy. Lepers were the outcasts of society. Most people feared infection from this deadly disease and would not go near them. But when a leper came to Jesus asking to be healed, Jesus touched him and healed him (Matt. 8).

## AVERTING DISASTERS

The miracles of Jesus demonstrated His authority over all the areas of darkness that bring misery to human lives. On one occasion, the disciples of Jesus were caught in a storm that blew up while they were rowing across the lake. Jesus rebuked the wind, and the lake became completely calm. The disciples were astonished. "Who is this?" they asked. "Even the wind and the waves obey him!" (Mark 4:41).

## DELIVERING THE OPPRESSED

Jesus also delivered people from demonic oppression. When He came to the area of the Gerasenes, a deranged man rushed toward Him. Demons had made themselves at home in this man, bringing terrible destruction to him and everyone around him. He lived in graveyards, where he would cut his own body. Nobody could control him, and he was a violent threat to the nearby community.

When Jesus saw the man, He commanded the evil spirits to come out of him. And at the command of Jesus, the demons departed. When the local people came to see what had happened, they found the man sitting dressed and in his right mind (Mark 5).

### RAISING THE DEAD

The authority of Jesus extended beyond sickness, nature, and the demonic. He even controlled the realm of death. On three occasions He brought the dead back to life. The apostle John records the story of how Lazarus, a friend of Jesus, died. Four days after he was laid in a tomb, Jesus raised him from the dead. Jesus stood by the tomb and called Lazarus to come out. And he came out—walking in the bandages they had wrapped round his body (John 11).

*A View from the Second Mountain*

Jesus' miracles were more than dramatic interventions. They were signs revealing His authority and confirming His identity. When John the Baptist questioned whether Jesus was really the Messiah, Jesus said, "The blind receive sight, the lame walk, those who have leprosy are cleansed, the deaf hear, the dead are raised, and the good news is proclaimed to the poor" (Matt. 11:5).

The miracles of Jesus were like flashes of lightning in

a dark sky. Jesus has authority over disease, disasters, demons, and death. He cares about the poor, and He has come to bring God's promised blessing in which our old debts will be canceled and our lost inheritance restored.

The miracles give a sample of the blessing that God has in store for all His people. But it is only a sample. Jesus did not eradicate blindness or leprosy. The local hospital did not close in Jerusalem. Undertakers did not go out of business. To discover why, we must travel through the next valley.

*Chapter 13*

---

# **opposed**

**REACTION TO JESUS** was decidedly mixed. His miracles and teaching brought great joy to many people, but His claims stirred up deep resentment and opposition in others.

Jesus' dramatic announcement of Himself as the Messiah turned a quiet worship service in the synagogue at Nazareth into a riot as the congregation drove Him out of His own hometown (Luke 4:28–32). As far as they were concerned, He was Joseph's son. They regarded His claim as blasphemous, and from that day, He was no longer welcome in their town.

## PLEASE GO AWAY!

Something similar happened when Jesus delivered the man who had been possessed by evil spirits in the Gerasenes. Instead of welcoming Jesus to their town and seeking His help with other problems, the local people pleaded with Jesus to leave the area! So He got in a boat and left.

When Jesus healed the man who had been blind from birth, the man's neighbors brought him to the Pharisees. Instead of praising God for the miracle, they threw him out of the synagogue, and this became their standard procedure for anyone who acknowledged that Jesus was the Christ (John 9:22).

## THE ROOTS OF OPPOSITION

Opposition to Jesus centered on His unique and extraordinary claims. Only God gives life, only God raises the dead, and only God pronounces final judgment. And Jesus claimed that these rights belong to Him! "Whatever the Father does," He said, "the Son also does. . . . For just as the Father raises the dead and gives them life, even so the Son gives life to whom he is pleased to give it.

Moreover, the Father judges no one, but has entrusted all judgment to the Son, that all may honor the Son just as they honor the Father" (John 5:19–23).

Jesus was claiming that every person who has ever lived is ultimately accountable to Him. There was no ambiguity in His words. Jesus was "calling God his own Father, making himself equal with God" (5:18). These claims cause deep offense in every culture. So it should not surprise us that "for this reason [the Jews] tried all the more to kill him" (5:18).

The Pharisees felt that in opposing Jesus they were upholding the Old Testament, but Jesus claimed that they had missed the whole point of the Old Testament because it all spoke of Him. "You study the Scriptures diligently because you think that in them you have eternal life," He said. "These are the very Scriptures that testify about me, yet you refuse to come to me to have life. . . . If you believed Moses, you would believe me, for he wrote about me. But since you do not believe what he wrote, how are you going to believe what I say?" (5:39–40, 46–47).

## USING THE DEVIL'S POWER

The depth of antagonism toward Jesus became clear when the Pharisees accused Him of working miracles by the power of the devil. Jesus had just delivered a man who had been possessed by a demon. The Pharisees could not deny the miracle that everybody had just seen. They needed an explanation, so they told the people, "It is only by Beelzebul, the prince of demons, that this fellow drives out demons" (Matt. 12:24).

It was an extraordinary accusation. Satan's strongholds were falling as people who were obviously possessed by demons were set free. If Jesus was doing this by the power of Satan, then Satan would be destroying his own kingdom (12:26)!

Jesus turned the argument on the Pharisees by asking them about the power with which their people drove out demons. The question was embarrassing to the Pharisees because they were unable to help people who were oppressed by dark powers.

Jesus cast out demons by the power of the Spirit of God, and this, He claimed, was another evidence that God's kingdom, His liberating rule, had come (12:28).

People were deeply divided over the claims and miracles of Jesus. But there was no avoiding a decision. Jesus offered a clear choice: "Whoever is not with me is against me" (12:30).

## STONES IN THE TEMPLE

On another occasion, Jesus was teaching in the temple at Jerusalem. "I am the light of the world. Whoever follows me will never walk in darkness, but will have the light of life" (John 8:12). As He spoke, many people put their faith in Him, and He continued to teach them. "If you hold to my teaching, you are really my disciples," He said. "Then you will know the truth, and the truth will set you free" (8:31–32).

The suggestion that they needed Jesus to set them free offended these new believers. "We are Abraham's descendants and have never been slaves of anyone," they said (8:33).

A long conversation followed about God's promises to Abraham and his descendants. Then Jesus said, "Your father Abraham rejoiced at the thought of seeing my day; he saw it and was glad" (8:56).

The people were astonished at this claim. "You are not yet fifty years old, . . . and you have seen Abraham!" (8:57).

"Very truly I tell you," Jesus answered, "before Abraham was born, I am!" (8:58).

In these words, Jesus identified Himself fully with the God of Abraham, Isaac, and Jacob, who had appeared to Moses and revealed His own name as "I AM" (Ex. 3:14). When the people heard these words from Jesus, they picked up stones to stone Him. But Jesus slipped away from the temple grounds (John 8:59).

## A View from the Second Valley

The deep antagonism and hatred shown toward Jesus was a great tragedy. Imagine what good might have been done in Nazareth, in the land of the Gerasenes, or in the great city of Jerusalem if Jesus had been welcomed and invited to stay.

The apostle John summarized the pattern of opposition

to Jesus in these words: "He came to that which was his own, but his own did not receive him" (John 1:11). This response did not surprise Jesus. "This is the verdict," He said, "light has come into the world, but people loved darkness instead of light because their deeds were evil" (John 3:19).

But some did receive Jesus. They followed Him and saw His glory. Their story takes us to the next mountain.

*Chapter 14*

---

# transfigured

**JESUS' CENTRAL MESSAGE** was clear and simple: "The kingdom of God has come near. Repent and believe the good news!" (Mark 1:15). A kingdom is a place under the rule of a king, and when Jesus spoke about "the kingdom of God," He was speaking about the blessings of life under the rule of God.

Those who live under God's rule belong to His kingdom, and Jesus made it clear that this privilege is open to all. The condition of entrance is that you repent and believe the good news. You cannot enjoy the benefits of the kingdom if you will not bow to the King.

## THE FAITH OF THE APOSTLES

Jesus invited many people to follow Him, but He designated twelve of them to be His apostles. Their special role was to be with Jesus, to preach, and to cast out demons (Mark 3:14–15). They were privileged to see Jesus' miracles and to record what He said and did.

As they traveled with Jesus, He taught them to obey God, to love one another, and to live a life of faith under the rule of God.

When Jesus was alone with these disciples, He asked them, "Who do you say I am?" (Matt. 16:15). Peter stepped forward and spoke for the others: "You are the Messiah, the Son of the living God" (16:16). After three years with Jesus, the disciples were convinced that He was the Promised One to whom the whole of the Old Testament had pointed.

Jesus chose this moment to tell His disciples what lay ahead: "The Son of Man must suffer many things and be rejected by the elders, the chief priests and the teachers of the law, and he must be killed and on the third day be raised to life" (Luke 9:22).

Jesus knew what lay ahead of Him. The suffering He

endured on the cross did not take Him by surprise. He was prepared for it. He had come "to give his life as a ransom for many" (Mark 10:45), and He went to Jerusalem to fulfill that purpose.

## A GLIMPSE OF THE FUTURE

About a week later, Jesus took three of His disciples on a prayer retreat. They climbed a mountain together, and when they arrived at the top, Jesus gave Peter, James, and John a glimpse of the future. While Jesus was praying, "the appearance of his face changed, and his clothes became as bright as a flash of lightning" (Luke 9:29).

An awesome brilliance radiated from Jesus, and it is clear that the three disciples were at the limits of vocabulary to describe how He looked. Mark records Peter's recollection, saying that Jesus' clothes appeared "whiter than anyone in the world could bleach them" (Mark 9:3).

We call this event the Transfiguration. Jesus was showing His disciples the glory that He would enter after His death and resurrection. The disciples needed to see this. In the next few days, they would see the face of Jesus battered, bruised, scourged, and beaten. He would be so disfigured as to become unrecognizable (Isa. 52:14).

A crown of thorns would be forced onto His head. And after six hours of hanging on the cross, the light in His face would go out, and His eyes would be darkened in death. The disciples needed to know that this would not be the end, so Jesus gave them a glimpse of the glory that lay beyond the cross.

Two men, Moses and Elijah, appeared with Jesus. They shared in the glory that was radiating from Him. This must have been completely astonishing to the disciples. Fifteen hundred years had passed since the death of Moses, and about seven hundred since the death of Elijah, and yet here they were sharing in the glorious splendor of Jesus.

It was more than the disciples could take in at the time, but it was the clearest indication that death would not be the end for Jesus or for His people. Great glory lay ahead.

### THE AWESOME CLOUD

But the most dramatic moment in this whole experience was still to come. As the disciples were talking with Jesus, a cloud enveloped them. They immediately recognized what was happening. The presence of almighty God had come down to Mount Sinai in a cloud when He gave the Ten Commandments to Moses. The same cloud of God's presence had filled the temple in the days of Solomon. Now the cloud of God's presence was coming to them. The disciples were terrified and fell on the ground, until Jesus lifted them up (Matt. 17:6–7).

When God came down to meet with Moses at Mount Sinai, He spoke with an audible voice. Now the audible voice of God was heard again: "A voice came from the cloud, saying, 'This is my Son, whom I have chosen; listen to him'" (Luke 9:35).

### A View from the Third Mountain

The disciples could not have asked for a clearer vindication of their faith in the Lord Jesus Christ. They had seen the pattern of opposition to Jesus from people who claimed to be experts in the Law of Moses. But now they had seen Moses himself appearing as a direct witness to the claims of Jesus.

More than that, God the Father had spoken in an audible voice, affirming that Jesus is indeed His Son and directing the disciples to listen to Him. Some regarded Jesus as a great teacher, a miracle worker, or a prophet. Others dismissed Him as demon possessed. But God the Father affirmed Him as His Son.

Later, the apostle John wrote these words about Jesus: "The Word became flesh and made his dwelling among us. We have seen his glory, the glory of the one and only Son, who came from the Father, full of grace and truth" (John 1:14).

The glory of the Transfiguration prepared Jesus and the disciples for what lay ahead in Jerusalem. That story takes us into another dark valley.

*Chapter 15*

---

# **suffered**

**JUDAS DECIDED TO BETRAY** Jesus after a party. A woman had poured expensive perfume over Jesus' feet. It was a lavish gift and a beautiful expression of love. Jesus saw it as an act of worship. The disciples saw it as a waste of money. And it was after this event that Judas, one of the twelve apostles, went to the chief priests and negotiated a fee of thirty pieces of silver to betray Jesus (Matt. 26:14–16).

The night before He was crucified, Jesus shared a meal with His disciples. "I have eagerly desired to eat this Passover with you before I suffer," He said (Luke 22:15). Judas was at the table, and Jesus reached out to him in love. "One of you is going to betray me," He said (John 13:21). John asked Jesus who would do such a thing, and Jesus told him it would be the person to whom He gave the bread. Then Jesus offered the bread to Judas, who took it and left the room, going out into the night (John 13:22–30).

## AGONY IN THE GARDEN

After the meal, Jesus went with His three closest disciples into a garden called Gethsemane, where He faced the full horror of the suffering that lay ahead. "My soul is overwhelmed with sorrow to the point of death," He said (Matt. 26:38). Then He went to pray alone.

In a deep agony of spirit, Jesus cried out to the Father, "If it is possible, may this cup be taken from me. Yet not as I will, but as you will" (26:39). Then, in a conclusive act of commitment to the Father, He said, "If it is not possible for this cup to be taken away unless I drink it, may your will be done" (26:42).

After He had finished praying, Jesus returned to the three disciples who had fallen asleep. At that moment, Judas arrived, leading a large crowd armed with swords and clubs. When Judas identified Him, Jesus was arrested and taken to the home of Caiaphas, the high priest.

All the disciples abandoned Jesus and fled. He was utterly alone as He entered the beginning of His suffering.

### "WHO HIT YOU?"

The events that took place in the house of Caiaphas were a strange mixture of a trial and an interrogation. The high priest placed Jesus under oath.

"Tell us if you are the Messiah, the Son of God," he demanded (Matt. 26:63).

"You have said so," Jesus replied (26:64).

That answer ignited the fury of the high priest. Caiaphas accused Jesus of blasphemy, and the seventy members of the ruling council pronounced Jesus worthy of death. Then, gathering round Jesus, they spat in His face and struck Him with their fists. They blindfolded Jesus and took turns striking Him. "Prophesy. . . . Who hit you?" they said (26:68).

## CALLING DOWN CURSES

While all this was going on, Peter had come to the courtyard outside the high priest's house. Someone who had been with Judas in the garden recognized Peter as a follower of Jesus and challenged him (John 18:26).

Peter erupted in anger, calling down curses on himself and swearing that he did not know Jesus. Peter's violent language expressed what he felt. He wished with all his heart that he had never had anything to do with Jesus.

At that very moment Jesus was dragged from the high priest's house across the courtyard. Covered in spittle and bruised from many blows, He heard the voice of His friend Peter cursing, swearing, and vowing that he had never known Jesus.

Jesus turned and looked straight at Peter as he was speaking (Luke 22:61). Peter's denial must have wounded Jesus more than any of the blows in the high priest's house.

## MAINTAINING LAW AND ORDER

Caiaphas handed Jesus over to Pilate, the Roman governor who had the authority to sentence Jesus to death. Pilate was convinced that there was no basis for a charge against Jesus, and so in an attempt to avoid making a decision, he sent Jesus to King Herod. But Herod sent Him back.

Pilate called the chief priests together and told them, "You brought me this man as one who was inciting the people to rebellion. I have examined him in your presence and have found no basis for your charges against him. Neither has Herod, for he sent him back to us; as you can see, he has done nothing to deserve death" (Luke 23:14–15).

At this point, the crowd that had gathered began chanting and calling for Jesus to be crucified. Pilate's duty was to uphold law and order. But there was no law and there was no order in his actions, only the worst kind of self-interest. Pilate knew that Jesus was innocent, but the people were calling for His death, and Pilate feared a riot. So he handed Jesus over.

## A CROWN FOR THE KING

There was deep hatred in the vicious cruelty poured out on Jesus. First, He was flogged. A leather lash studded with pieces of bone lacerated His back.

Then He was stripped. Soldiers dressed Him in a scarlet robe and began to mock Him. Christ had claimed to be King, so they decided to give Him a crown. Someone cut down some branches from a thorn bush, twisted them together, and forced them onto His head. They put a reed in His hand and knelt down in mockery, saying, "Hail, king of the Jews" (Matt. 27:29; Mark 15:18; John 19:3). They spat on Him, and then they took the reed and struck Him on the head repeatedly.

The brutality of this extended torture was such that the face of Jesus was disfigured beyond recognition (see Isa. 52:14). And after all this abuse, they led Jesus away to be crucified.

*A View from the Third Valley*

The sufferings of Jesus show the depth of hatred toward God hidden inside human hearts. The deepest problem of human nature is not our ignorance about God but our rebellion against God. If Jesus came to our culture today, we would crucify Him all over again. We would not use a cross and nails. We would do it with ridicule on talk shows. The hatred would be the same.

Jesus suffered at the hands of human beings. He came to us, and we crucified Him. That shows the depth of the human sinfulness in which we all have some share.

*Chapter 16*

---

# crucified

**IF EVER THERE WAS A TIME** when you might expect the judgment of God to fall from heaven, it would be the moment when Jesus was nailed to the cross. God took on our human flesh and came among us in Jesus Christ. And we crucified Him. The world was on a collision course with God.

What happened next was truly remarkable. As Jesus was nailed to the cross, He said, "Father, forgive them, for they do not know what they are doing" (Luke 23:34). There was no thunderbolt from heaven, no lightning strike of God's judgment. The soldiers who tortured Jesus went home to their families. Pilate woke up the next morning. Caiaphas continued as high priest. Forgiveness and mercy were released. The light of hope was shining in the middle of the most appalling hatred and violence.

## MOCKING AND TAUNTING

A crowd gathered around the cross of Jesus to watch Him suffer. They taunted Jesus about His claim to be the Son of God. "Come down from the cross, if you are the Son of God," they said. "Let God rescue him now if he wants him" (Matt. 27:40, 43).

The soldiers joined in mocking Jesus. If He couldn't do anything to save Himself from the awful suffering He was experiencing, what could He possibly do to save other people?

Two robbers who were crucified beside Jesus joined in heaping insults on Him (Matt. 27:38; Mark 15:32). But then something changed.

One of the thieves stopped shouting. A deep silence seemed to come over his soul as he realized his true position. He was approaching the last moments of his life. Earth was receding, and eternity was looming on the horizon. Soon he would stand in the presence of God, and he realized that he was not prepared.

"Don't you fear God . . . ?" he asked his friend, who continued to shout insults toward Jesus. "We are punished justly, for we are getting what our deeds deserve. But this man has done nothing wrong" (Luke 23:40–41).

The thief accepted responsibility for his own actions. He recognized that the long arm of the law had caught up with him and that he was receiving justice. But he also saw that Jesus was suffering a great miscarriage of justice. And he knew enough about God to believe that somewhere beyond death Jesus would be vindicated.

## A COURAGEOUS REQUEST

Spurred on by these thoughts, the thief turned toward Jesus. Above Jesus' head was an inscription that read "THE KING OF THE JEWS" (Matt. 27:37). It was obvious that if Jesus were to rule a kingdom, it would not be in this world. He was only a few hours from death. But beyond death, there is eternity, and that awesome reality was now filling the thief's mind.

"Jesus," he said, "remember me when you come into

your kingdom" (Luke 23:42). He recognized that Jesus had the authority of a king, and he believed that Jesus might be able to help him.

The thief had no idea of when this would happen. But perhaps in eternity Jesus would recall the unusual circumstances of their meeting. And if Jesus remembered him, perhaps there could be some hope.

It was a courageous request. The crowd had mocked Jesus' claim to save others. But the thief felt that Jesus was the one person who might be able to help him. So he stood out from the crowd and staked his hope on Jesus.

## AN IMMEDIATE PROMISE

Christ's reply was immediate. "Truly I tell you," He said, "today you will be with me in paradise" (Luke 23:43).

Paradise! This was far more than the thief could ever have dreamed. Paradise was the place where the blessing and presence of God would be known. Jesus was about to enter that blessing. He would take the believing thief with Him. And it would happen "today"!

This must have come as a shock to the thief whose best hope was for some help in the distant future. But Jesus made it clear that death would not lead this man into a long period of unconsciousness or a process of preparation. Death would lead into the immediate presence of God, and Jesus promised that He personally would bring this man into paradise. Suddenly, this man, for whom the world held nothing, found that, because of Jesus, he was about to enter the greatest joy a human being can ever know.

## IT'S NEVER TOO LATE

The story of the thief who was saved in the last hours of his life helps us to identify the clear steps by which any person can come to Jesus:

1. The thief recognized his own sinful condition. He realized that he had broken God's Law. He made no excuses or evasions.
2. He asked Jesus to help him.
3. And Jesus answered with a simple promise that the thief believed. He was saved by faith in a crucified Savior.

Whatever you have done or failed to do, you can come to Jesus in the same way. Recognize your sinful condition. Believe in the Lord Jesus Christ. Ask Him to save you. It is never too late to come to Him.

*A View from the Fourth Mountain*

We have described the crucifixion as a mountain rather than a valley because the glory of the Lord Jesus Christ was revealed on the cross. Forgiveness, grace, and mercy were poured out as Jesus prayed for His torturers and opened paradise for a repentant criminal who had no other hope.

We have traced the story of Jesus' suffering at the hands of men and His ministry of compassion even in the extremity of His pain. But there is another dimension of the story. The Bible makes it clear that in His death, Jesus bore the guilt and punishment for our sins. To understand what this meant for Jesus, we must now explore the deepest and darkest valley in the entire Bible story.

*Chapter 17*

---

# forsaken

**THE CROWD HURLED ABUSE** at Jesus for three hours, and then something wholly unexpected happened: "At noon, darkness came over the whole land until three in the afternoon" (Mark 15:33).

Jesus had said, "I am the light of the world" (John 8:12; 9:5). When men chose to extinguish that light, God covered the land with darkness. And the events that took place in these three hours of darkness take us to the heart of the Bible story.

## THE SACRIFICE

In Old Testament times, God's people performed a yearly ritual in which the high priest placed his hands on a goat and confessed the sins of the people over the head of the animal. God told the priest to put the sins of the people on the goat's head (Lev. 16:21). The ritual was an illustration of how God would remove our guilt by transferring it to another place.

This theme runs throughout the Bible. The Old Testament prophet Isaiah spoke about the sufferings of the Messiah and said, "The LORD has laid on him the iniquity of us all" (Isa. 53:6). God placed our sins on the Messiah, and He carried them as if they were His own.

In the New Testament, John the Baptist identified Jesus as "the Lamb of God, who takes away the sin of the world" (John 1:29). He would accomplish what all the Old Testament sacrifices had illustrated.

The apostle Peter described what happened to Jesus in the darkness in these words: "'He himself bore our sins' in his body on the cross" (1 Peter 2:24). The apostle Paul put it this way: "God made him who had no sin to be sin for us" (2 Cor. 5:21).

The whole Bible bears witness to this central, mysterious, and wonderful truth, that Jesus bore the guilt of our sins in His death on the cross.

It is not surprising that God shrouded this awesome event in darkness. Try to picture your sin as a load that you carry. God the Father lifted that load and placed it on Jesus, who carried it for you. Jesus died bearing the sins of the world. We cannot begin to imagine what that meant to the holy Son of God.

## HELL ON EARTH

When Jesus carried our sins, He also endured every dimension of the consequences they bring. The perfect Son of God became the guilty one in the eyes of the Father, and Jesus experienced the full force of sin's punishment poured out on Him.

Sin separates us from God, and during these awful hours of darkness, the comfort of the Father's love was taken from the Son. Christ entered into all the dimensions of hell on the cross, and from the depth of His agony He cried out in a loud voice, "My God, my God, why have you forsaken me?" (Matt. 27:46).

Jesus was the lightning rod for God's judgment. By absorbing the full force of the penalty of human sin in His own body, He opened the way for others to be saved from the judgment of God. He had prayed that others would be forgiven, and through His death, He made this possible.

This is a moment to pause and worship. We cannot fathom what the cross must have meant to God the Father and God the Son. What must it have been like for the Father to give up the Son for us? What must it have been like for the Son to be plunged into the depths of hell?

## MISSION ACCOMPLISHED

After three hours, the darkness passed, and Jesus cried out, "It is finished" (John 19:30). These words were a declaration of triumph. The storm was over. The judgment poured out on Christ was exhausted, fully spent. Everything that needed to be done to reconcile men and women to God had been accomplished. Sin had been dealt with, justice had been satisfied, and Jesus had completed everything that the Father had given Him to do.

Now all that remained was for Jesus to lay down His

life. He called out with a loud voice, "Father, into your hands I commit my spirit" (Luke 23:46). The life of Jesus was not taken from Him (John 10:18). He gave Himself for us (Gal. 2:20).

## "THE SON OF GOD"

A centurion and several of his men had been posted to guard the cross of Jesus. Their task was to make sure that nobody could save Jesus from death. They had guarded the cross throughout the entire six hours of Jesus' crucifixion and had witnessed everything that happened.

Earlier, the soldiers had joined with the crowd in taunting Jesus. But the sudden, unnatural darkness at midday silenced everyone. Then, at the moment Jesus died, the earth began to shake. The sudden darkness followed by the earthquake terrified the soldiers standing at the foot of the cross, and they confessed, "Surely he was the Son of God!" (Matt. 27:54).

The crowd who had watched Jesus suffer and die went home in shock and horror. They had been convinced that they were honoring God by crucifying Jesus. But nobody could doubt that the hand of God had been in the darkness and the earthquake (Luke 23:48). What would the future hold if they had crucified the Son of God?

*A View from the Darkest Valley*

The day that Jesus died was the darkest day in human history. Lifted up on a cross, Jesus was suspended between earth and heaven, rejected by the one and forsaken by the other. But we call this day Good Friday, because everything God had promised to do since the beginning of time was accomplished by the death of the Lord Jesus Christ on the cross.

Bearing our sin, He made it possible for us to be righteous before God. Being forsaken by the Father, He opened the way for us to be reconciled to God. Entering into the depths of hell, He opened the way into heaven.

The unfathomable suffering of Jesus in the darkness is the lowest point in the Bible story. But the deepest valley leads directly to the highest mountain.

*Chapter 18*

---

# risen

**AFTER THE DEATH OF JESUS**, two members of the Jewish ruling council openly confessed their faith in Him. Joseph of Arimathea had been a secret follower of Jesus, and he had not consented to the decision of the Sanhedrin to put Jesus to death (Luke 23:50–51). He was joined by Nicodemus, who had also been deeply impressed but had kept his faith secret for fear of what others might think (John 19:39).

These two men went to Pilate, and Joseph asked for the body of Jesus. It was Friday evening, and they wanted to bury the body before the Sabbath.

Pilate was cautious. His first response was to ask for

confirmation that Jesus was in fact dead. The centurion who had guarded the cross confirmed the fact without reservation. Then Pilate released the body.

Joseph owned a tomb in a garden near the place where Jesus had been crucified, so they laid the body of Jesus there and rolled a stone against the entrance to the tomb.

### TOP SECURITY

The following morning, a delegation of chief priests and Pharisees went to Pilate. They knew that Jesus had said He would rise after three days, and they wanted to make sure that the tomb was guarded so that there was no possibility of the disciples stealing the body.

Pilate told the Pharisees to "take a guard" and "make the tomb as secure as [they] knew how" (Matt. 27:65).

### AN EMPTY TOMB

The following morning, some women who had followed Jesus went to visit the tomb. They were astonished to find that the stone had been removed from the entrance. They looked inside—and saw that the tomb was empty.

Key moments in the Bible story are usually accompanied by supernatural events. Angels filled the sky when Jesus was born, so it should not surprise us that angels announced the news of Jesus' resurrection from the dead.

Sitting on the stone that had sealed the tomb, an angel of the Lord said to the women, "Do not be afraid, for I know that you are looking for Jesus, who was crucified. He is not here; he has risen, just as he said" (Matt. 28:5–6).

## THE RISEN CHRIST

The good news announced by the angel was not that "Jesus is alive" but that "He is risen." It is worth thinking about the difference. The Son of God was alive in heaven before He ever took human flesh. So why did He not simply leave His crucified body in the tomb and return to the Father? After all, it was only flesh and bone. Why did He bother with it?

The angels could still have appeared on Easter Sunday morning and said, "His body is here in the tomb, but don't worry, His spirit is with the Father in heaven." After all, is this not precisely what we say at a funeral service when a Christian dies? We bury the body and then we say,

"Although the body of our dear departed brother is here, his soul is with the Father in heaven."

But the angel did not say that about Jesus. The message is that Christ is risen. It was not just the spirit of Jesus that was delivered from death—but also His body.

## VICTORY OVER DEATH

God has joined the soul and the body together. Death separates them. That is why it is such a terrible enemy. It is the undoing of our nature. Death would not be defeated by the survival of the soul. Victory over death will be achieved only when the body and the soul are reunited in the power of a new life. And that is precisely what happened when Jesus rose from the dead.

The Bible places great emphasis on the physical nature of the resurrection. When Jesus appeared to the disciples, they thought they were seeing a ghost. Jesus wanted them to know that what they were seeing was more than the spirit of Christ in a visible form, so He said to them, "Touch me and see; a ghost does not have flesh and bones, as you see I have" (Luke 24:39).

The flesh that lay in the tomb had been raised. The

good news was not that the spirit of Jesus had survived death and lived on, but that the body of Jesus was raised from the dead. Jesus had come through death and triumphed over it.

## *RISEN* MEANS CHANGED

When the body of Jesus was raised, it was also changed. This was something that had never happened before. Jesus brought Lazarus back from the dead, but Lazarus came out of the tomb exactly as he had gone into it. And he carried on the process of aging at the point where he had left off. Then at some point the poor fellow had to go through the whole miserable business of dying all over again.

But when Christ was raised, His body was no longer subject to aging, sickness, pain, or death. No longer limited by the restrictions of time and space, His flesh was transformed and adapted for eternity.

This is the glorious future that lies ahead of every Christian believer. Since Christ has been raised, we also will be raised. When Christ returns, He will gather all His people into His presence. Every believer will be there, not only in mind but also in body. God has determined to redeem not just a part of you but the whole of you.

The greatest delights of body and soul in this life are only a hint of what God is preparing for those who love Him. Believing more clearly in the resurrection of the body will give you a stronger anticipation of life in heaven.

*A View from the Fifth Mountain*

Christians do more than follow the words of an ancient teacher. They share the life of a risen Savior. Jesus said, "I am the resurrection and the life. The one who believes in me will live, even though they die" (John 11:25). The resurrection of Jesus vindicated His claim and His promise.

If you find it hard to believe in the resurrection of Jesus, you may find it helpful to know that even the first disciples had doubts. The story of their journey to faith takes us into the next valley.

*Chapter 19*

# doubted

**THE GOSPELS DO NOT** hide the doubts of the first believers. When the women found the empty tomb of Jesus, they were completely lost for an explanation. They certainly did not think Jesus had risen from the dead. The idea did not even occur to them (Luke 24:4–8).

These women had believed in Jesus. They followed Him and shared a deep love for Him. But they had been traumatized by the horrible reality of His excruciating death, which they had witnessed just two days before. Their visit to the tomb was motivated by love, but it was absolutely devoid of faith. Their hopes and dreams had been shattered.

## THE DISCIPLES WHO DID NOT BELIEVE

The trauma of great suffering and loss has led some people to say with sadness that they can no longer believe. That was precisely the position of these women on the first Easter morning.

The empty tomb left them wondering until God gave them the explanation. Two angels appeared and announced to them that Jesus had risen (Luke 24:6–7). Then the women remembered Jesus' promise and believed (24:8). Christian faith does not rest on feelings, impulses, or personal insights. It rests entirely on grasping and believing what God tells us He has done. If God had not told them why the tomb was empty, they would never have known what to make of it.

The women returned from the tomb and told the disciples what had happened. But the disciples did not believe them (24:11). Peter raced to the tomb and saw the strips of linen cloth, but he still left "wondering to himself what had happened" (24:12). It was only when Jesus appeared to the disciples that their hearts gladly embraced what their minds could no longer deny.

## IRREFUTABLE EVIDENCE

Thomas was not with the other disciples when Jesus appeared to them, and he insisted that he would not believe unless he had irrefutable physical evidence: "Unless I see the nail marks in his hands and put my finger where the nails were, and put my hand into his side, I will not believe" (John 20:25).

Thomas loved and respected the other disciples, but he refused to rest his faith on the experience of his friends. He was determined that his faith should rest on solid evidence.

One week later, the disciples were gathered in the house again, and Thomas was with them. Jesus came to them and spoke directly to Thomas. "Put your finger here; see my hands," He said. "Reach out your hand and put it into my side. Stop doubting and believe" (John 20:27).

Faced with the evidence he had asked for, Thomas believed and confessed his faith in Jesus, his Lord and God.

## SEEING AND BELIEVING

The faith of the apostles was a believing response to the evidence placed before them. They saw. And because they saw, they believed. This theme runs throughout the Gospel accounts of the resurrection. When John went into the empty tomb, he saw and believed (John 20:8). Mary Magdalene told the disciples, "I have seen the Lord!" (20:18). Jesus showed His hands and His feet, and "the disciples were overjoyed when they saw the Lord" (20:20).

The apostles were given the unique role of being direct witnesses to the resurrection. A witness is someone who has seen an event directly, not someone who can report things secondhand. This was so important that when the apostles chose a replacement for Judas it had to be someone who was a direct witness of the resurrection (Acts 1:22).

So Thomas was right to insist that he had to see Jesus for himself. Hearing reports from the others was not enough if he were to fulfill the role of an apostle.

### HOW CAN WE BELIEVE?

The Bible's emphasis on seeing raises an obvious question: How can we who have not seen Jesus believe? The answer is that the four Gospels present us with the evidence of eyewitnesses to the life, death, and resurrection of Jesus.

The unique calling of the apostles was to record and proclaim what they had seen and heard about Jesus so that people in every generation and culture would have the opportunity to believe.

God has not called us to a blind faith. He invites us to investigate the claims of Jesus, and He presents us with the evidence of His words and works in the Gospels so that we may do so.

## A RELATIONSHIP OF INTEGRITY

Christian faith is a believing response to the evidence God has placed before us. It does not rest on the dogmatic assertions of the church, or on the mystical experiences of an individual, but on the evidence of God's Word, the Scriptures.

God has created you with a mind, a heart, and a will, and He will not bypass any of them. He invites you into a relationship with Himself that has integrity because your mind is persuaded, your heart is captivated, and your will is committed.

This does not mean that all your questions will be answered. But it does mean that God has given sufficient evidence for you to "believe that Jesus is the Messiah, the Son of God, and that by believing you may have life in his name" (John 20:31).

# V

## *A View from the Fifth Valley*

Faith belongs in the valley rather than on the mountaintop because there are many things that we cannot see. We walk by faith, not by sight. And that means we live with many unanswered questions.

Christian faith affirms what God has revealed. Christian humility admits there are many things we do not know. But faith in Jesus stands on a sure foundation of solid evidence, and those who trust in Him will not be disappointed.

After the resurrection, Jesus appeared to the disciples and other believers over a period of forty days. On the last of these occasions, they caught a glimpse of what Jesus had promised for the future. That story takes us to the last great mountain peak in this second stage of our journey.

*Chapter 20*

---

# ascended

**OVER A PERIOD OF FORTY** days after the resurrection, Jesus taught His disciples and brought them to a new level of understanding. Previously, they had thought of the cross as an unmitigated disaster. Now, they saw that everything had happened exactly as God had planned it.

Christ was not with them constantly throughout these forty days. He appeared to them, He taught them, and then He disappeared. In this way, He began to wean them away from dependence on His physical presence.

For three years they had been used to talking with Jesus directly, face-to-face. But now things would be different.

They would have to learn to follow Jesus by faith and not by sight. Gradually, they became used to trusting Jesus without seeing Him.

## THE GREAT COMMISSION

At the end of the forty days, Jesus went to the Mount of Olives with His disciples. He commissioned them to "go and make disciples of all nations" and promised them His continuing presence (Matt. 28:18–20). But their immediate instructions were to wait in Jerusalem.

Jesus had taught them about the Holy Spirit. Now He promised that the Spirit would come and give them power to be His witnesses to the ends of the earth (Acts 1:8).

Then Jesus ascended into heaven. On other occasions when Christ had appeared, He had simply vanished. But this time, they saw Him go. This was the end of the resurrection appearances to the disciples. The evidence had been given; the training was complete. And now Jesus was returning to the Father.

## INTO THE CLOUD

Luke records that Jesus "was taken up before their very eyes, and a cloud hid him from their sight" (Acts 1:9). God made His presence known in a cloud at critical moments in the Bible story. The cloud filled Solomon's temple, giving the people a visible sign of God's presence. In the story of the Transfiguration, God spoke from a cloud on the mountain.

Now, as Jesus ascended, the disciples saw that He was received into the cloud. Could anything be clearer than this? The same Christ who had come from the Father was now returning to the Father. Having finished His work, He was received by the Father, represented in the cloud.

## A MAN IN HEAVEN

The disciples were filled with joy when Jesus left them because they knew that He had returned to the Father (see Luke 24:52). This meant that for the first time in human history, there was a man in heaven.

Adam was expelled from God's presence, and as a result, all his children were alienated from God. Christ was received into the Father's presence, and as a result, all who follow Him will be welcomed by the Father. Adam led us out. Jesus leads us in.

The disciples knew that Jesus would represent them before the Father. The Son of God assumed our humanity on earth, and He has taken it into heaven, where He acts as an advocate for His people.

## THE JOY OF SITTING DOWN

When Jesus ascended to the Father, "he sat down at the right hand of the Majesty in heaven" (Heb. 1:3). This phrase is full of significance. The priests in the Old Testament never sat down. The furniture in the temple included a lamp and a table but no chair. The absence of a chair was a visual reminder that the priest's work was never done. There was always another sacrifice to be made.

But Christ's work is finished. There is no more sacrifice to be offered, no more atonement to be made, nothing more that needs to be done to placate the wrath of God and release forgiveness to His people. Christ's redeeming work is complete, and that is why He sat down.

## THE BLESSING THAT NEVER ENDS

Last impressions usually make a powerful impact on the mind, and the last glimpse the disciples had of Jesus was full of significance. Jesus lifted up His hands and blessed the disciples, and "*while he was blessing them*, he left them and was taken up into heaven" (Luke 24:51, emphasis added).

The disciples watched Jesus ascend into the cloud, still speaking God's blessing into their lives. He hadn't finished blessing them! Today the ascended Lord Jesus Christ continues what He was doing when the Father took Him up into the cloud: pouring out His blessing into the lives of His people. Every good gift in your life comes from His hand.

## THE PROMISE OF HIS RETURN

Jesus spoke plainly to His disciples about His return: "I will come back and take you to be with me that you also may be where I am" (John 14:3).

As Jesus ascended, two angels confirmed this promise. "This same Jesus, who has been taken from you into heaven, will come back in the same way you have seen him go," they said (Acts 1:11).

Jesus had spoken to Caiaphas about a day when he would "see the Son of Man sitting at the right hand of the Mighty One and coming on the clouds of heaven" (Matt. 26:64). Caiaphas regarded this as blasphemy. But God the Father vindicated Jesus by raising Him from the dead. One day, every person who has ever lived will see Jesus in His full glory. For His friends, it will be the beginning of great joy. For His enemies, it will be the beginning of unending sorrow.

What happened to Jesus in His ascension will happen for all His people when He comes in glory. Just as Jesus was snatched up into the cloud, so when He returns all who believe in Him will be caught up to meet Him in the air. Every Christian will participate in that day. Those who have already died will not miss out. They will come with Him, and from that moment all of Christ's people will be forever with the Lord (1 Thess. 4:17).

*A View from the Sixth Mountain*

The disciples went back to Jerusalem with joy. They were just a handful of people, and they faced a monumental task. How could they possibly fulfill the commission to make disciples of all nations? The answer lay in the person and work of the Holy Spirit.

*Chapter 21*

---

# waiting

**THE DISCIPLES RETURNED** to Jerusalem reflecting on all that they had experienced and anticipating all that lay ahead. Jesus had told them to wait in Jerusalem until they received the promised gift of the Holy Spirit. "John baptized with water," He said, "but in a few days you will be baptized with the Holy Spirit" (Acts 1:5).

The word *baptize* literally means "to dip" or "to drench." In the early church, believers were baptized in rivers. They were either plunged under the water or water was poured over their heads.

Jesus said that a baptism was to be given "in the name of the Father and of the Son and of the Holy Spirit"

(Matt. 28:19). Baptism is a picture of the Christian life, which is all about being drenched in the Father, plunged into the Son, and soaked in the Spirit.

The Father, the Son, and the Holy Spirit permeate every part of a believer's life. You cannot separate one from the others. The Spirit draws you to the Son. The Son brings you to the Father. The Father and the Son pour out the Spirit into your heart. No one can know the Father apart from the Son, and no one can come to the Son except by the Spirit.

## RESPONDING TO A MYSTERY

The Bible makes clear that there is one God and that He is Father, Son, and Holy Spirit. We cannot fathom the nature of God, and that is not surprising. I assume that fish have a very limited understanding of human nature, and in a similar way, it is beyond the range of human ingenuity to figure out the nature of God.

The nature of God may be a mystery, but it is not a contradiction. It would be a contradiction if Christians believed that there is one God and that there are three

Gods. But to say that there is one God who exists in three persons is not a contradiction; it is a mystery.

The way to respond to this mystery is to let it lead you to worship. You will never be able to figure out the mystery of the nature of God, but you can gaze in wonder at the unfathomable splendor of the one eternal God who is Father, Son, and Holy Spirit.

## THE MINISTRY OF THE SPIRIT

Jesus told His disciples that after He ascended into heaven, His presence would be with them by the Holy Spirit. The new situation offered one wonderful advantage: the presence of Jesus would now be with each of His disciples at all times and in every place. This is what Jesus was referring to when He said, "It is for your good that I am going away. Unless I go away, the Advocate will not come to you; but if I go, I will send him to you" (John 16:7).

Jesus told His disciples that the Holy Spirit would be "with" them and "in" them (John 14:17). These descriptions are important. The word *with* speaks of companionship. The Holy Spirit is a person. There are two distinct identities here, and we must never confuse them. A person who fails to distinguish between himself or herself and the Holy Spirit is on the road to fanaticism and deception.

## MORE THAN A MENTOR

But Jesus also said that the Holy Spirit would be "in" His disciples. The Holy Spirit is more than a mentor who shows us what to do. If we are to live the Christian life, we need more than advice and encouragement. We need the presence and power of God to work within us.

The ministry of the Holy Spirit goes beyond the work of a pastor, friend, coach, or counselor who may be able to shed light on problems and suggest possible ways forward. The Holy Spirit works *in* us. He is able to touch the deep places of your soul, renewing your mind, redirecting the affections of the heart, molding and reshaping the will, cleansing the imagination, and healing the memory.

The Holy Spirit can create new desires within you to follow Christ, not out of a sense of duty but from a heart that hungers and thirsts for righteousness. He can give you the power to live a new life for the glory of God.

## SIGNED, SEALED, AND DELIVERED

Through His death and resurrection, Jesus has opened the way for sinful men and women to be reconciled to God and to enter everlasting life. This is the promise of God. It has been signed by the Father and sealed by the blood of Christ. But what has been signed and sealed still needs to be delivered.

Today, the Holy Spirit takes what Jesus has accomplished on the cross and applies it personally to us. He takes what Christ has made possible for all people and makes it a reality for you (John 15:26; 16:14).

If the Son of God had not come, you could not be saved. If the Spirit of God had not come, you *would* not be saved. Without the work of the Holy Spirit, salvation would remain a possibility for all of us, but it would never become a reality for any of us. If there were no Holy Spirit, nobody would arrive in heaven, and all that Jesus accomplished on the cross would be like a gift that was purchased but never received.

## *A View from the Sixth Valley*

The disciples had experienced the power and presence of the Holy Spirit as Jesus had sent them out in ministry. But the Holy Spirit had not yet been given (John 7:39). Jesus told the disciples to wait in Jerusalem for the gift that the Father had promised and that Jesus had spoken about.

They did not have to wait long. Just ten days after Jesus ascended into heaven, and fifty days after the resurrection, there was a festival called Pentecost. The story of what happened on that day takes us to the beginning of a whole new range of mountains.

PART THREE

# Living in
## *the Spirit*

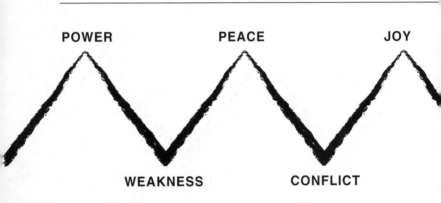

POWER          PEACE          JOY

WEAKNESS          CONFLICT

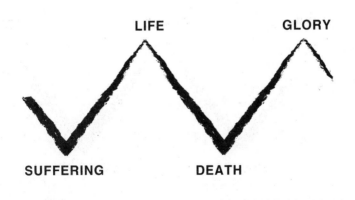

LIFE        GLORY

SUFFERING        DEATH

**THE FINAL STAGE OF** our journey will take us through Acts and the letters of the New Testament, where we discover the highs and lows of the Christian life.

If you belong to the Lord Jesus Christ, you have peace with God, the power to live a new life, and the joy of knowing that Christ is able to keep you in every circumstance of life. The life of God is in you, and you are destined for eternity in the presence of Jesus. These are the mountains.

But the Christian life also has its deep valleys. You will feel your own weakness. You will find yourself engaged in an unending conflict with sin. You will experience trials, discouragement, and setbacks, and one day you will die.

I have called this section "Living in the Spirit" because God has given His Holy Spirit to every believer. God's Spirit is with us and in us as we walk up the mountains and through the valleys.

Our journey through the Old Testament and the Gospels presented a narrative in which each story built on what had gone before. In this third stage of our journey, the order of the chapters is not important—except, of course, that death and ultimate glory come at the end!

The experiences described in these mountains and valleys run throughout the entire course of the Christian life. The paradox is that we have power and yet experience weakness. We have joy and yet experience sorrow. We know peace and yet find ourselves in conflict.

This final stage of our journey offers an inside look at the experience of a Christian. These chapters will give you the opportunity to test your expectations, measure your experience, and renew your focus on the final destination, which is the goal of our journey.

*Chapter 22*

# power

**IN THE ENTIRE CITY OF** Jerusalem, there were only about 120 believers in Jesus (Acts 1:15). The task of reaching their community seemed to be beyond them. There was very little money, very few people, a lot of fear, and a culture that had very little room for their message. The challenge Jesus had given them to make disciples of all nations must have seemed impossible.

But Christ had spoken about an event that would change all that. In a few days they would be "baptized with the Holy Spirit" (1:5). Then He added, "You will receive power . . . and you will be my witnesses in Jerusalem, and in all Judea and Samaria, and to the ends of the earth" (1:8).

They did not have to wait long. Just ten days after Jesus ascended into heaven, the Holy Spirit was poured out on the first Christian believers. After that, things were never the same.

## THE BLOWING WIND

While the believers were gathered together, "a sound like the blowing of a violent wind came from heaven and filled the whole house where they were sitting" (Acts 2:2).

When Jesus appeared to His disciples after the resurrection, John tells us that "he breathed on them and said, 'Receive the Holy Spirit'" (John 20:22). Jesus was explaining what would happen on the day of Pentecost. He was saying to His disciples, "This is what it will be like. I am going to ascend to heaven, and when I do, I will breathe my life into you from above." Then He took a deep breath and blew it out toward them.

So when the disciples heard a sound like the rushing wind just a few days later, they would have associated it with the sound of Jesus breathing on them and recognized that this was the fulfillment of what Jesus had promised.

Of course, the Spirit of God had been at work in the lives of believers before. The Holy Spirit came on many individuals in the Old Testament, anointing them for specific tasks, and the disciples' experience before Pentecost would have been similar. But this was something entirely new. The Spirit of God was not only with them, but in them.

### THE FIRE THAT DID NOT BURN

The believers, gathered in the upper room, "saw what seemed to be tongues of fire that separated and came to rest on each of them" (Acts 2:3). This must have been absolutely terrifying.

A great fireball or pillar of fire came toward them. As it came nearer, it divided into individual flames that rested on every person in the room. The astonishing thing was that none of them was burned.

Something like this had happened before, when God spoke to Moses from a fire that rested on a bush but did not burn it (Ex. 3:2). God promised that His presence would be with Moses, and on the day of Pentecost, God gave this same sign of His presence to the first believers. They would have remembered how God spoke from the fire and commissioned Moses. But they must have wondered who the fire would rest on now. Would it be Peter, or perhaps James and John? Perhaps it could be all three of them.

But the ball of fire separated into flames that rested on each of the believers. God was commissioning every believer to advance His purpose in the world. Each one was gifted and equipped for ministry.

### CROSS-CULTURAL COMMUNICATION

A third remarkable event followed the wind and the fire. Suddenly and spontaneously, the believers found that they were able to speak in languages they had never learned (Acts 2:4).

This was a complete reversal of what happened at the Tower of Babel (Gen. 11). Early in the Bible story, God broke the momentum of man's rebellion by introducing multiple languages into the human race. In the confusion and alienation that followed, people were scattered to the north, south, east, and west.

At Pentecost, people "from every nation under heaven" had gathered in Jerusalem (Acts 2:5). When God enabled the believers to speak spontaneously in languages they had never learned, people from the whole world—north, south, east, and west—heard and understood the good news of Jesus Christ.

A large crowd had gathered, and Peter spoke to them about the death and resurrection of Jesus. God had exalted Jesus, and now He had poured out the promised Holy Spirit on His people. This was the explanation of what the crowd was seeing and hearing.

Three thousand people responded to Peter's message, confessing their faith in Jesus through baptism. When they returned to their homes, they took the good news of Jesus to the cities and nations from which they had come.

God had promised that His blessing would come to people from all nations. The stream of God's blessing began with one man, Abraham. Now the river of God's mercy burst its banks and flooded out to all the nations of the world.

## *A View from the First Mountain*

The story of Pentecost teaches us that the Holy Spirit of God is given to every believer. If you belong to Christ, God's life is in you, His presence is with you, and His blessing is upon you.

The Holy Spirit equips and empowers all believers for service and ministry. In the past, God had worked through a few people who were anointed for special ministries, but now the Holy Spirit lives in and works through all believers.

God calls us to communicate the good news of Jesus across cultural and linguistic barriers so that His blessing will flow to people from every tribe, language, and nation on the face of the earth. Every Christian has a part to play in that purpose. When you step out in obedience to that calling, you will begin to experience your weakness.

*Chapter 23*

---

# weakness

**AFTER PENTECOST**, the new believers quickly established four priorities: learning from the apostles' teaching, growing in fellowship, breaking bread together, and praying (Acts 2:42).

The first believers were all Jewish, and in the earliest days, they met in the courts of the temple and in homes. The depth of their commitment to each other was demonstrated as they sold their possessions and gave to people in need. God performed many miracles through the apostles, and the believers enjoyed wide support across the city of Jerusalem.

## A PATTERN OF PERSECUTION

The temple authorities took a different view. They arrested Peter and John and brought them before Caiaphas, who had interrogated and condemned Jesus. The ruling council instructed the apostles not to speak or teach in the name of Jesus. Peter and John responded by saying that they could not stop speaking about what they had "seen and heard" (Acts 4:20).

Later, all the apostles were arrested. And when that did not stop them, the ruling council had them flogged. It was their first taste of what would become a pattern of persecution.

As the number of believers continued to grow, they appointed leaders to oversee the ministry so that the apostles could devote themselves to prayer and preaching the Word of God (6:2–4).

Stephen was the first man chosen for this work, and he became the target of a group who wanted to destroy the community of believers. He was arrested and tried on false charges (6:9–14), just as Jesus had been before. He gave a marvelous defense of his faith, but before he could finish, he was dragged out of the city and stoned (Acts 7). Stephen became the first Christian martyr, the first of many who have given their lives in serving the Lord Jesus Christ.

Stephen's death was the beginning of a wave of persecution against the early believers, who left Jerusalem and scattered (8:1). One especially zealous Pharisee by the name of Saul was determined to hunt them down. With the support of the high priest, he set out to pursue them. The first city that he targeted was Damascus.

## THE APOSTLE TO THE GENTILES

It was on the road to Damascus that Christ intercepted Saul's life. He was blinded by a brilliant light, and he heard a voice asking, "Saul, Saul, why do you persecute me?" (Acts 9:4). Confronted directly by the risen Lord Jesus, the whole direction of his life turned around, and the greatest enemy of the church became its greatest champion. We know him better as the apostle Paul.

Like most of the first believers, Paul was a Jew. But God commissioned him to take the good news of Jesus to the Gentile world. And it was through Paul's missionary journeys that churches were planted throughout the Roman Empire.

God spoke to Paul directly, just as He had spoken to the prophets in the Old Testament. The New Testament includes thirteen of his letters, beginning with the book of Romans to which we will turn in the next chapter.

## NO STRANGER TO SUFFERING

You might think that a person so uniquely used by God and empowered by the Holy Spirit would live a life of constant triumph, but Paul spoke candidly about his experience of weakness. His testimony gives us an insight into one of the deep valleys of the Christian life.

Paul was no stranger to suffering. On five occasions he endured thirty-nine lashes. Three times he was beaten with rods. Once he was stoned. And three times he was shipwrecked (2 Cor. 11:24–25). Constantly on the move, he faced danger wherever he went. This man was no wimp.

Paul endured something that was deeply painful in his life, which he describes as his "thorn in [the] flesh" (2 Cor. 12:7). We don't know what this was, but knowing Paul's courage, we can be confident that it was no minor irritation.

He pleaded with God for relief from this problem,

but God did not give him what he asked. Instead, God gave him this promise: "My grace is sufficient for you, for my power is made perfect in weakness" (2 Cor. 12:9). The mark of true spirituality is not that God gives you everything you ask, but that you walk with Him when He does not.

## THE PRESSURES OF MINISTRY

The reason Paul experienced weakness was not that he lacked courage or stamina. It was that God had put him in situations that pushed him well beyond the boundaries of his own comfort. He knew what it was to feel utterly, unbearably crushed, and at one point he "despaired of life itself" (2 Cor. 1:8; see also 11:28–29).

Those who throw themselves into the work of Christian ministry will soon experience the weakness that Paul knew. As you follow Christ, you will experience times of discouragement and even exhaustion. You will face unanswered questions and problems that seem to have no resolution.

But this weakness is not something to be afraid of or ashamed of. Paul saw his experiences of weakness as opportunities because this was where Christ's power rested on him (12:9). It will be the same for you.

In Christian ministry, strength that knows itself to be strength is actually weakness, and weakness that knows itself to be weakness in God's hand is strength. That is why Paul said, "For Christ's sake, I delight in weaknesses, in insults, in hardships, in persecutions, in difficulties. For when I am weak, then I am strong" (12:10).

*A View from the First Valley*

Never imagine that your feeling of weakness means that you are out of the will of God. If you wait until you feel confident before you move forward in what God is calling you to do, you may never get to it.

Jesus did not live within cautiously safe limits. When He says, "Follow Me," He calls us beyond ourselves and leads us outside our comfort zones. A person who knows only his strength and not his weakness has not followed far.

God often puts us in situations where we know that we

are out of our depth so that we will learn to depend on Him. When you experience weakness, Christ's power will rest on you. And it will be obvious that what you accomplish has been done by God.

*Chapter 24*

---

# peace

**PAUL'S ENCOUNTER WITH** Jesus on the road to Damascus was the turning point of his life. Jesus confronted him with a single life-changing question: "Saul, Saul, why do you persecute me?" (Acts 9:4).

Saul had persecuted Christians because he was on a collision course with God. But through his encounter with Jesus, he discovered the priceless gift of peace with God. How this peace can be yours is a central theme in the New Testament.

Paul explained what happened to him, and to all of Christ's followers, in these words: "Since we have been justified through faith, we have peace with God through our Lord Jesus Christ" (Rom. 5:1). The gift of peace with God comes from Christ. It belongs to those who are justified and it is received by faith. These great themes take us to the summit of our second mountain.

## BALLS AND STRIKES

In a game of baseball, the umpire decides whether the pitcher has thrown a ball or a strike. The opinion of the crowd or the TV commentators is irrelevant. The umpire decides. Similarly, in a court of law, the judge decides whether a defendant is guilty or innocent. The attorneys present their case, but the judge decides. His declaration is final.

The word *justified* describes a decision or declaration that a person is in the right. Its opposite is the word *condemned*, which describes a decision or declaration that a person is in the wrong.

One day, every person who has ever lived will stand before God. On that day, God will announce who is in the right and who is in the wrong. God will make the declaration. Other opinions will be irrelevant.

Since the Bible declares clearly and repeatedly that all

people have sinned and fall short of God's standard, this is not an attractive prospect. So when we read about how we can be justified, or declared right by God, we have every reason to explore how this is possible.

## HOW CAN WHAT'S WRONG BE RIGHT?

The good news is that God justifies sinners (Rom. 4:5). But this statement obviously raises a problem. Declaring sinners to be "in the right" looks like a miscarriage of justice. How could God do that? The answer to that question is: "Through Jesus Christ."

When Jesus died on the cross, God the Father laid the guilt and punishment for our sins on Him (Rom. 3:25; 1 Peter 2:24). Justice demands that sin should be punished, and God demonstrated His justice by passing our sentence on Jesus. Jesus served the sentence for our wrongdoing. Justice was done.

The law of double jeopardy makes it clear that a person cannot be charged twice for the same crime. So if our sins have been paid for by Jesus, there is no way that they can be charged against us, either now or in the future. This is why "there is now no condemnation for those who are in Christ Jesus" (Rom. 8:1).

If God justifies people through the death of Jesus Christ, then we must discover how the benefits of Jesus' death can be applied to us. The answer to that question is: "Through faith."

## HOW CAN TWO BECOME ONE?

Imagine a young couple who meet on a blind date. Over the course of time, they develop a friendship, and then they fall in love. Eventually they find themselves making vows to each other as they are joined together in marriage.

This is a helpful picture of the way in which faith joins us to Jesus Christ. Like any other relationship, faith in Jesus begins when you discover who He is. That is what we have been doing in our journey through the Bible. But faith involves more than learning about Jesus. Knowing about another person does not make a marriage, and knowing about Jesus does not make Him ours.

In the marriage service, the groom is asked if he will take the bride to be his wife. Then the bride is asked if she will take the groom to be her husband. A marriage is formed when the bride and groom commit to each other in love.

Our union with Christ works the same way. Two thousand years ago, Jesus was asked if He would take you and become your Savior. Would He bear your sins? Pay your debts? Endure your hell? And on the cross, Jesus Christ answered "I will" to all these questions.

Now God has a question for you: "Will you take Jesus Christ as Savior and Lord of your life? Will you commit yourself wholly and fully to Him?" Faith answers "I will" to these questions, and when that answer is given, a bond of union is formed between you and Jesus.

### THE GIFT OF SHALOM

Everything that Jesus accomplished on the cross becomes yours by faith. God counts your sins as being dealt with in His death. Your case is closed. There are no charges for you to answer. You are justified through faith in the Lord Jesus Christ, and in this way you have peace with God (Rom. 5:1).

The Hebrew term for *peace* is the beautiful word *shalom*. It is one of the most common Jewish greetings, and it means "May things be the way they ought to be." When you are justified by faith through the Lord Jesus Christ, things are as they ought to be between you and God. "We have peace with God" (Rom. 5:1)

*A View from the Second Mountain*

Peace with God does not mean that you will be free from conflict. Every Christian is involved in a lifelong struggle against sin in his or her life, and we have already seen that the early believers faced hostility and persecution on account of their faith in Jesus.

Jesus spoke directly to this issue. He said to His disciples, "I have told you these things, so that in me you may have peace." But immediately He went on to say, "In this world you will have trouble" (John 16:33). So the peace Jesus spoke about is not the absence of trouble or conflict in our lives.

Jesus made it clear that the disciples would have peace and trouble at the same time. To discover more of what that looks like, we need to pass through another valley.

*Chapter 25*

---

# conflict

**PAUL KNEW WHAT IT WAS** like to struggle with sin both before and after his life-changing encounter with Jesus. "I find this law at work," he said. "Although I want to do good, evil is right there with me" (Rom. 7:21).

Looking back on his earlier experience, he recalled how his good desires were constantly frustrated by another impulse that he did not fully understand. He felt like a prisoner, unable to lead the life that he wanted to live, and this made him miserable. "What a wretched man I am!" he said. "Who will rescue me from this body that is subject to death?" (7:24).

Trying harder was not the answer. Paul knew that

temptation was more powerful than he was. He needed help, and when he came to faith in Jesus Christ, he found it. That is why he answered his question, "Who will rescue me?" with the triumphant reply, "Thanks be to God, who delivers me through Jesus Christ our Lord!" (7:25).

## A FIGHT THAT IS NOT FINISHED

Becoming a Christian does not mean that your battle with sin and temptation is over.

When you come to Christ, you become a new person. Your new life is lived by faith in the Son of God, but it is also a life in the body (Gal. 2:20). That's why it is such a struggle! As long as you are in the body, you will experience the pull of temptation. There is no avoiding this battle.

The roots of sin lie so deep within us that even when we come to Christ they are not taken away. Temptation is still around us, and impulses to sin remain within us. Paul refers to these as "the misdeeds of the body" (Rom. 8:13), the "acts of the flesh" (Gal. 5:19), or "deeds of the flesh" (NASB); they are "whatever belongs to your earthly nature" or to "your old self" (Col. 3:5; Eph. 4:22).

The flesh is like a bubbling spring that constantly

throws up new ways of displeasing God. It is like a raging fire that keeps throwing up sparks, and each stage of life has its own special pitfalls. It is easy to imagine that the conflict is over when one temptation recedes, but that is never the case. The old nature will go on, suggesting new thoughts, words, and actions that are displeasing to God throughout the entire course of your life.

You need to know that your struggle with sin is not a sign of failure. It is the normal experience of an authentic Christian. The Christian is like a fish swimming against the flow of the river. The struggle is a sure sign that you are heading in the right direction. The only alternative is to go with the flow.

## GOING ON THE OFFENSIVE

God calls every Christian to take the initiative in launching an active assault against sin in our lives. We are to go on the offensive against anything in our thoughts, words, or actions that is displeasing to God:

> *Put to death . . . whatever belongs to your earthly nature. (Col. 3:5)*

*Put off your old self, which is being corrupted by its deceitful desires. (Eph. 4:22)*

*If by the Spirit you put to death the misdeeds of the body, you will live. (Rom. 8:13)*

Paul's violent and aggressive language reflects the teaching of Jesus about dealing with sin in our lives. "If your eye causes you to stumble," He said, "gouge it out and throw it away" (Matt. 18:9). Obviously, Jesus was not commanding self-mutilation, but He did make it clear that we must take radical action against sin in our lives.

Our first reaction to these commands may be to look at temptations that have overwhelmed us in the past and to protest that we are not able to do this. But the Scriptures always speak to the Christian believer as someone who has the power to take action. God has put you in a position to fight. The Holy Spirit is given to every person who belongs to Jesus, and by His power you are able not only to engage in this struggle but also to win it: "Sin shall no longer be your master" (Rom. 6:14).

## IDENTIFYING THE ENEMIES

The Scriptures give specific examples of the kinds of sins we are to fight against in our thoughts, words, and actions.

Sins in our thoughts include impurity, lust, idolatry, evil desires, greed, anger, bitterness, jealousy, and selfish ambition. Sins in our words include slander, malice, and filthy language. Sins in our actions include sexual immorality, rage, witchcraft, drunkenness, brawling, discord, factions, and orgies (Col. 3:5, 8; Eph. 4:29; Gal. 5:19–21).

There is no room for any of these things in the life of a Christian believer. God calls us to get rid of them. We are to give them no quarter.

Please don't muddy the waters by saying that you can't help it. If you can't help it, then come to the risen Lord Jesus Christ in faith and He will deliver you. If you have come to Christ, then His power is at work in you.

Don't say that you can't overcome temptation. Without Christ you would be a prisoner of sin. With Christ you are empowered and equipped for battle.

*A View from the Second Valley*

The struggle against sin is your responsibility. God will not fight this battle for you, but He will fight it with you.

God has called you to engage in the struggle, and He has equipped you for it. Imagine a fully armed soldier walking on patrol. Suddenly, an enemy comes running toward him. The soldier uses the equipment he has been given and takes action to cut the enemy off before the enemy can destroy him.

Temptations will keep coming at you, and God calls you to cut them off before they destroy you. He has equipped you for this battle. By the power and presence of the Holy Spirit, He has put you in a position to fight and to win.

*Chapter 26*

---

# joy

**MAYBE YOU ARE NOT** sure whether you will ultimately make it to heaven. You hope that you will, but sometimes you wonder whether your faith is strong enough or your repentance deep enough.

So it is important for us to leave the valley of conflict and climb to the next mountain where we can glimpse the ultimate victory that is promised to every believer in Jesus Christ.

One day, the struggle of your Christian life will be over. You will stand in the presence of Jesus. You will see His face, and when you see Him, you will be like Him (1 John 3:2).

## GOD'S GLORY IN YOU

God's promise is not just that you will be brought into the glory of His presence but also that His glory will be revealed in you. Paul says, "I consider that our present sufferings are not worth comparing with the glory that will be revealed in us" (Rom. 8:18). Notice, he does not say "to us" but "in us." God's glory will be in you!

The Holy Spirit is already creating some reflection of God's glory in the life of every believer. We "are being transformed into his image with ever-increasing glory, which comes from the Lord, who is the Spirit" (2 Cor. 3:18).

The process has begun, and one day it will be complete. Those who have been justified will be glorified (Rom. 8:30). God will finish what He has started in your life, and when His work in you is complete, you will not be disappointed.

When we pass through the valleys of weakness, conflict, and suffering, we need the confidence of knowing the ultimate outcome of all that God is doing in our lives. That is the joy that sustains us. "We rejoice in hope of the glory of God" (Rom. 5:2 ESV).

## HOW CAN YOU BE SURE?

How can you be sure that you will make it to heaven? You may have started the Christian life, but how do you know that you will finish? If we do not know how to answer these questions, they will soon take away our joy.

Satan loves to remind us of the many hazards that lie in the valleys of the Christian life, and we can only rejoice in the hope of ultimate victory if we are confident that God will bring us through.

## INADEQUATE ANSWERS

If I were to ask you how you know you will spend eternity in heaven, how would you answer?

One answer might be "Because I love Christ." That's great, but how deep is your love? Is it always shown in obeying His commandments? You can't stand with confidence on your love for Christ.

Another answer might be "I have made a commitment." That's wonderful. But what happens if your commitment weakens? Would that mean that your chances of entering heaven would diminish too? You can't stand with confidence on your commitment to Christ.

A third answer might be "I have faith." Again, that's marvelous. But how strong is your faith? Are there not times when you struggle with doubt? You can't stand with confidence on your faith in Christ.

The common factor in these three inadequate answers is the little word *I*: "I love Christ"; "I am committed"; "I have faith." And the problem with anything that begins with *I* is that it is never complete, never what it could be, and never what it should be.

## THE BLOOD OF JESUS

That's why we should be supremely thankful that entrance into heaven does not depend on our faith, our commitment, our works, our love, or anything in us, but on the blood of our Lord Jesus Christ. "Since we have now been justified by his blood," the Bible declares, "how much more shall we be saved from God's wrath through him" (Rom. 5:9).

If my salvation depended on the strength of my faith or the depth of my love, I could never know what the outcome of my life would be. But the final outcome does not rest on these things. It rests on the blood of Jesus. This is our solid ground for humble and joyful confidence: we are "justified by his blood."

## SOLID GROUND

Picture two scenes. In the first, a confident person steps out on a lake covered in ice. The ice is thin. His confidence is misplaced, and he goes down. In the second, a very nervous person moves hesitantly onto solid ice. She moves slowly because she is afraid that the ice might break. But she has nothing to fear. The ice is thick. Her safety does not depend on the strength of her faith but on the strength of the ice.

Your salvation does not depend on the strength of your faith but on the strength of your Savior.

If you want to cultivate a confident and joyful anticipation of heaven, the question to ask is not "How strong is my faith?" or "How warm is my heart?" or "How deep is my commitment?" These questions keep you looking at yourself, and that will only raise more questions!

Instead ask, "Is the blood of Jesus Christ rich enough and strong enough to wash away every sin and to cover every weakness, failure, and inadequacy in my life from now until the day I arrive in the presence of God?" The answer to that question is "Absolutely, without question or hesitation, yes!"

### *A View from the Third Mountain*

Jesus Christ died to save you, He lives to keep you, and He will never let you go (Rom. 8:32–39). That's why you do not need to worry about what the future holds. Whatever comes, He will be with you, and He will bring you through.

What event in life could ever separate you from the love of Christ? What power in hell could stop what He is doing in your life? God gave His Son to die for you, and you can be supremely confident that nothing will stop Him from bringing you all the way to heaven.

*Chapter 27*

---

# suffering

**BAD THINGS HAPPEN TO** good people. Sometimes terrible things happen to wonderful people, and God allows it to be so.

Perhaps you have felt that if you pursue a godly life, you could expect God to keep you from significant suffering. But there is no such deal on the table. Christian faith does not inoculate us against suffering in a fallen world.

The greatest and most godly person who ever lived suffered more than any other. He was rejected by His family. He wept at the graveside of one of His dearest friends. He was betrayed. He suffered injustice. And He was crucified. He calls us to walk in His footsteps, and He tells us clearly, "In this world you will have trouble" (John 16:33). God never promised a pain-free path to heaven.

## FALSE CLAIMS AND EXPECTATIONS

From its earliest days, the church has been troubled by teachers who offer more than God has promised. They describe Christian experience as mountains without valleys, but a message that ignores the valleys is not big enough for life. It raises false expectations, and it has nothing to say to a suffering world.

Every Christian walks through the valley of suffering. Your suffering may involve physical pain, loss, stress, illness, betrayal, disappointment, injustice, or even abuse. Believers have faced all of these in the valley of suffering. Paul speaks about trouble, hardship, persecution, famine, nakedness, danger, and sword (Rom. 8:35). And when you walk through your valley, you need to know what God says about your experience.

## SUFFERING HAS MEANING

The first thing God wants you to know about suffering is that it is not meaningless. "We know," Paul writes, "that suffering produces perseverance" (Rom. 5:3). Our troubles "are achieving for us an eternal glory that far outweighs them all" (2 Cor. 4:17). Something comes of your suffering. It produces. It achieves. Our first instinct in pain is to feel that it is pointless, but God tells us it never is.

Think of a bulb being planted. You dig a hole in the dirt, place the bulb in the hole, and then you cover it with dirt and mulch. Imagine the process from the bulb's perspective! If the bulb could talk, it would say, "I've been dumped on. I am surrounded by dirt. I cannot see the light of day." But the bulb has life in it. That life presses up toward the light, and the dirt that buried the bulb ends up contributing to its growth.

Your faith will be dumped on in many painful experiences, but true faith is like a living seed that pushes upward. God wants you to know that the trials that threaten to bury you will be the means by which you grow.

## PASSING THE TEST

Trials are also the means by which your faith is proved genuine. Suffering produces perseverance, and perseverance produces character (Rom. 5:4). When you persevere through the valley of suffering, you show that your faith is authentic (1 Peter 1:7).

I will always remember an evening when about twenty members of our congregation met to share their stories of loss. Each of them had experienced the death of a son or daughter.

We spoke at length about unanswered questions and unresolved pain, but at the end of the evening one thing stood out to me more than any other. Here were twenty people who had experienced inexpressible pain. Their suffering remained a mystery, and yet they still loved Christ.

The greatest evidence of the true work of God in the human heart is that, when God allows a person to suffer, he or she loves Him still. God's people love Him for who He is, not simply for what He gives.

Your response to God in times of trouble will be one of the most revealing things about you. The true character of authentic faith is demonstrated in the valley of suffering.

## CHARACTER PRODUCES HOPE

Your journey through this valley will also lead you into hope (Rom. 5:4). Somewhere deep in every heart there is a dream of life as we would want it to be. Suffering reminds us that the dream can never be fulfilled in this fallen world. Our culture is sold out in the pursuit of paradise now. Suffering detaches us from that pursuit and directs our attention toward the day when there will be no more death or mourning or crying or pain, and when God will wipe every tear from our eyes (Rev. 21:4).

*A View from the Third Valley*

Imagine yourself putting together a jigsaw puzzle. Before you begin you are given three pieces of information: First, the manufacturers guarantee that all the pieces provided in the box belong to the same picture. Second, the manufacturer has not provided all the pieces. And third, the missing pieces will be provided when everything that can be done with the existing pieces is complete.

You tear the box open and start to put the pieces together. As your work progresses, you find some pieces exasperating; they don't connect with the work you have done, and they don't fit with each other.

Perhaps you have come to that place in your life. There is a piece that just doesn't seem to fit. You can't see how it could have any useful place in your life. You hate it and want to be rid of it, but without this strangely shaped piece, the picture cannot be completed.

One day, God will give you the other pieces. Then you will see where that which has caused you so much pain fits into the picture. And when that time comes, you will have more joy over that piece than all the others.

*Chapter 28*

# life

**WHEN A PERSON COMES TO** faith in Jesus Christ, the life of God enters his or her soul by the power of the Holy Spirit. Without this, the Christian life would be impossible. Somewhere in the valleys of weakness, conflict, and suffering, you would be overwhelmed.

Paul placed great emphasis on this when he wrote to Christians living in Colossae. They had been influenced by teachers who placed such strong emphasis on rules and self-discipline that they lost sight of the new life that God gives to every person who comes to faith in Jesus.

## THE PERSON YOU USED TO BE

When you came to faith in Jesus, the person you used to be ceased to exist: "If anyone is in Christ, the new creation has come: The old has gone, the new is here!" (2 Cor. 5:17). Putting it more bluntly, Paul wrote, "You died" (Col. 3:3).

This is good news, and it should come as a great relief. The Bible makes clear that the person you were before you came to Christ was alienated from God and unable to overcome the gravitational pull of sin (Eph. 2:3; 4:18). That person was in darkness, heading for the ultimate condemnation of God.

But when you came to faith in Jesus, that person died. Paul said, "I have been crucified with Christ and I no longer live" (Gal. 2:20). When you came to faith in Jesus, the person destined for God's judgment ceased to exist.

## THE NEW, RISEN YOU

God has made you a new person and given you a new identity in Jesus Christ. You are a new creation (2 Cor. 5:17). "You have been raised with Christ" (Col. 3:1). Christ lives in you (Gal. 2:20).

There is a big difference between painting a chicken on an egg and hatching a chicken from an egg. The painted chicken is artificial. It is imposed on the shell. The hatched chicken is alive. It is able to move and to function.

When you came to faith in Jesus, the Holy Spirit invaded your life. God made you alive and responsive to Him. You are a new person. The power of God is at work in you, giving you the ability to live the Christian life.

## THE PERSON YOU WILL BE

Your new life has begun, but it is not yet complete. "Your life is now hidden with Christ in God" (Col. 3:3). "What [you] will be has not yet been made known" (1 John 3:2). A tree looks bare in winter, but when spring comes, its life bursts out in a display of beauty. It is the same tree, but it is unrecognizably different.

That is how it will be with every Christian. God's life is in you, but its glory is hidden until Jesus comes again. It is winter now, but spring is coming. And when Christ appears, you "will appear with him in glory" (Col. 3:4).

One of the great joys of heaven will be to see and admire what God has done in the life of every believer.

## DON'T LISTEN TO FRED

This miracle of the new birth makes it possible to live the new life.

"Since, then, you have been raised with Christ," Paul says, "set your hearts on things above" (Col. 3:1). You have the power to set the prevailing affections of your heart. You can choose the things that you will love the most.

In the past, you were pushed around by impulses in your mind and your heart that were beyond your control. But now you are a new person. God has given you the ability to control your heart and mind, and this can take some getting used to.

Imagine that you have been working for the same boss for thirty years. Let's call him Fred. Every morning when you go to work, you check in with Fred, and he tells you what he wants you to do.

Then one day the owner of the company asks to see you. He says he has big plans for you. On Monday, you will have a new office, and you will serve in a new position.

As you arrive for the first day in your new job, you realize that you no longer have to take orders from Fred. Then it dawns on you that from now on, Fred will have to take orders from you. After thirty years, that will take some getting used to!

Two things are very likely to happen in the coming months. First, Fred will go on telling you what to do. He will always think of himself as your boss, even though that is no longer the case. Second, your natural instinct will be to listen to Fred and do what he tells you. You have thought of Fred as your boss for so long that it's hard to break the habit.

After six weeks in your new position, the owner asks to see you again. "There is a problem we need to talk about," he begins. "You are listening too much to Fred. If we had wanted him in charge, we would have given him the job. But we gave it to you.

"You have to adjust to the new situation," he continues. "Fred will always make suggestions, but you are under no obligation to pursue them. We have given you authority. Learn to use it. From now on, Fred does what you tell him."

God has put you in a new position of authority over

the impulses of your heart and mind. In the past, they pushed you around and told you what to do. But now you are in a position to give direction to your heart and your mind. Half the battle is knowing that you have the authority to do that.

## A View from the Fourth Mountain

If you want to live an effective Christian life, you must understand your new identity. The person you were before has ceased to exist. You are a new creation in Jesus Christ. God has placed you in a position of authority. Sin will always be your enemy, but it is no longer your master (Rom. 6:14).

When Christ appears, you will appear with Him in glory. But before we get to glory, there is one more valley that we have to cross.

## Chapter 29

# death

**WE HAVE ARRIVED AT** the last valley of the Christian life. The great mountain of God's eternal glory lies ahead, but the path that leads there runs through the shadowy valley of death. One day you will walk through this valley, and when you do, Christ will be with you.

When Jesus died, He changed the nature of death for every believer. We still have to walk through the valley, but death has no power over those who belong to Jesus.

The book of Hebrews explains what happened when Jesus died and how your death will be different as a result: "He suffered death, so that by the grace of God he might taste death for everyone" (Heb. 2:9).

Jesus was in great agony of soul as He prepared to face death. "My soul is overwhelmed with sorrow," He said in the garden of Gethsemane (Matt. 26:38). Overwhelmed!

Nothing else had overwhelmed Jesus. But as He anticipated His death, He said, "Father, if it is possible, may this cup be taken from me" (Matt. 26:39). The prospect of what He was about to experience filled Him with consternation. When you know what was in that cup, you will understand why He was appalled at the thought of drinking it.

## DYING A DOUBLE DEATH

The Bible speaks about death in two dimensions. The first, physical death, is familiar to us all. But there is also "the second death" (Rev. 2:11; 20:6, 14; 21:8). This is the judgment of God that will be poured out on the last day.

Jesus experienced both the first death and the second death simultaneously. Wicked men nailed Him to a cross, where life drained from His body. At the same time, God laid our sins on Jesus and poured out the judgment that was due to us on Him. So when we read that by the grace of God He tasted death for everyone, it means He tasted both dimensions of death together (Heb. 2:9).

Our Savior faced death as nobody else before or since has faced it. He endured death in both dimensions at the same time. And if facing that double death was so horrendous to Jesus in prospect, what must it have been like in reality?

Christian believers will never taste the second death. Christ endured it for us and drew its sting (1 Cor. 15:55). Death is still a dark valley, but its nature has been changed for every believer. That's what Jesus meant when He said, "Very truly I tell you, whoever obeys my word will never see death" (John 8:51). Christians face death without the sting. Your death will not mean separation from the Father but entrance into His presence.

## DON'T BE AFRAID

While many people die peacefully, some endure a great struggle. The prospect of dying can be frightening even for a person who is sure of his or her eternal destiny. So it is helpful to think about what will happen when you come to that moment of departure from this life.

The Gospels record an occasion when Jesus came to the

disciples who were in a boat on the lake. Late at night, Jesus went out to meet them, walking on the water. When the disciples saw Him, they thought He was a ghost, and they were terrified. But Jesus spoke to them. "Take courage! It is I. Don't be afraid" (Mark 6:50).

That's a great picture of what happens for the believer at the moment of death. Some Christians die peacefully and seem to have a strong sense of heaven being opened. Others die with a great struggle and, like the disciples, experience great fear. Either way, Jesus is coming to take them home.

## THE MOMENT OF ARRIVAL

The Bible gives us another wonderful picture of what death will be like for the believer. Viewed from this side of the valley, it is Christ coming to take us home, but viewed from heaven, it will be the moment of arrival.

When you arrive in heaven, Jesus will stand beside you and present you to the Father (Heb. 2:13). He has promised that if you confess Him before men, He will confess you before His Father in heaven (Matt. 10:32). Christ will gladly identify Himself with all His people. Before the Father He will say, "Here am I, and the children [you have] given me" (Heb. 2:13).

On that day, Christ's word will be the one thing that matters. He will confess you before the Father, and He will usher you into the joy of everlasting life. This is His promise, so what is there to fear?

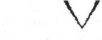

*A View from the Fourth Valley*

For the Christian believer, death is a passage into the immediate and conscious presence of Jesus. This gift is ours because Christ endured the second death for us. He drew the sting of death and changed its nature for all His people.

The experience of dying may be frightening, but Christ will walk with you through it, and He will bring you home. The Christian can say with assurance, "Though I walk through the valley of the shadow of death, I will fear no evil, for you are with me; your rod and your staff, they comfort me" (Ps. 23:4 ESV).

On the other side of the valley lies the great summit that is the destination of our journey. Its glory is beyond anything we have seen or can comprehend. But God has given us a glimpse of what's in store, and it is to that ultimate vision that we now turn.

*Chapter 30*

---

# glory

**WHILE THE APOSTLE JOHN** was imprisoned on the Isle of Patmos, God gave him a vision of the future, which John recorded in the book of Revelation.

John's vision gives us a glimpse of how world history will end and eternity begin. It is full of wonderful symbols that help us to grasp things that would otherwise be beyond our understanding.

John saw the evil that would be unleashed across history, especially in the last days. He saw the joy of Christ's people when they would be taken out of the suffering of this world and welcomed into Christ's presence. And he saw the final victory of Christ, when evil will be destroyed forever.

## A NEW HEAVEN AND EARTH

"Then," John wrote, "I saw 'a new heaven and a new earth,' for the first heaven and the first earth had passed away" (Rev. 21:1).

We can easily understand why God would make a new earth, but why would God make a new heaven?

Before there was ever rebellion on earth, there was rebellion in heaven. Satan wanted to ascend to the throne of God, and so he was cast out. The possibility of evil existed both on the earth and in heaven.

But now John sees that the enemy will be consigned to destruction forever and that God will shape a new heaven, free not only from the presence of evil but even from its possibility.

Then John says that he saw a "new earth." The destiny of the Christian believer is not a dreamlike existence in an imaginary world. God will reshape, re-create, replenish, and renew this planet: "The creation itself will be liberated from its bondage to decay" (Rom. 8:21).

At this point in the story, human history as we know it has been brought to a close. London, Chicago, Jerusalem, Cairo, Beijing, and Moscow are all gone! The earth has been laid bare in the fervent heat of God's judgment (2 Peter 3:10; Heb. 1:10–12).

John saw a new city coming down from heaven. He immediately recognized its skyline: Jerusalem! It was unmistakably familiar to him (Rev. 21:2).

## MEASURING THE CITY

Jerusalem is full of significance in the Bible story. This was the place where God came down to meet with His people when the cloud of His presence filled the temple.

The new city is absolutely vast. It is laid out like a square and measures 12,000 stadia—1,400 miles (Rev. 21:16)! The area covered by the city would be about three-quarters the size of America or five times the size of Great Britain.

John had already seen that the vast crowd of God's people were more than anyone could number. Now God was communicating that He has a place for every one of them.

The measurements of the city are given in three

dimensions. It is "as wide and high as it is long" (Rev. 21:16). In other words, it is a perfect cube.

John would have seen the significance of this immediately. The Most Holy Place in the temple, where God met with His people, was also a perfect cube: thirty feet long, thirty feet wide, and thirty feet high (1 Kings 6:20).

The old city had a holy place, where the presence of God came down. The new city *is* a holy place, where God's presence will remain. In the old Jerusalem, one room was filled with His glory. In the New Jerusalem, the whole city will be filled with His glory, and a vast crowd of men and women will live in God's presence forever.

## PARADISE RESTORED

At this point in the vision, John is invited to enter the city. As he enters—no doubt to his absolute astonishment—John sees a garden (Rev. 22:1–2)!

The Bible story began in a garden, and now, at the end of the Bible story, this paradise is restored. In the new garden, God's people have access to the Tree of Life, which bears twelve different crops of fruit, ready to pick every month. The variety of fruit speaks of the riches of life continually replenished in the presence of God.

The pleasures of God's new garden city will surpass anything Adam knew in the Garden of Eden. You will taste fruits Adam never tasted, and enjoy pleasures Adam never knew.

When you are in the presence of God, you will have no regrets. God will wipe every tear from your eyes (Rev. 21:4). Imagine God Himself doing that for you! Sometimes we may wonder how it would be possible to be in heaven and not to have tears for ourselves or for others. One thing is clear: God will remove not only our regrets but also the very source of them.

*A View from the Ultimate Mountain*

God's people will enjoy His presence in His great garden city. We will serve Him, and God says that we will "reign for ever and ever" (Rev. 22:5). Thankfully, this does not mean that we will all have government jobs.

When God speaks about us reigning, He is telling us that life will be ordered and brought under your control.

You will no longer be subject to the tyranny of time, piles of paperwork, and all that goes with it. You will no longer struggle with unpredictable tides of emotion, deceptions of the mind, or impulses of the will. You will no longer endure dysfunctional relationships, and you will no longer be subject to danger or death.

Your life will be ordered, your work fulfilled, and your relationships whole. Life itself will be brought under your control, and you will be free to fulfill all the purposes of God.

At the climax of his vision, John heard a voice from God's throne saying, "God's dwelling place is now among the people, and he will dwell with them" (Rev. 21:3). The alienation will be over. The curse will be gone. God's great purpose will be accomplished. And the life that He made you for will begin.

# An Invitation

**THE BIBLE ENDS WITH** a great invitation: "'Come!' Let the one who is thirsty come; and let the one who wishes take the free gift of the water of life" (Rev. 22:17).

The message of the Bible is that Jesus Christ offers the priceless gift of everlasting life to everyone who will come and receive.

Try to picture Jesus holding a gift in His hand and offering it to you. If this gift is to become yours, there must come a point where you take it from Him, and that is precisely what Jesus invites you to do: *Let the one who wishes take the free gift of the water of life.*

Picture yourself coming to Jesus with nothing to offer but everything to receive. He has what you need, and He offers it to you freely.

Faith is like a hand stretched out and open to receive. If you will come to Christ in faith, believing His promise, an act of transfer will take place in which the gift He offers will become yours and you will become His.

Why stand at a distance from the priceless gift that God offers to you?

***Prayer:***

*Almighty God,*

*I believe that Jesus Christ has purchased the gift of everlasting life through His death on the cross.*

*By faith I receive what He freely offers to me.*

*Forgive me for my many sins, and help me to live a new life that honors You.*

*Fill my heart with Your love, and lead me in Your paths.*

*Let me live for Your glory, through Jesus Christ my Lord, amen.*

# Index of Scriptures

**13. Opposed**
Matthew 12; 15:1–20
Mark 3:20–35; 7
Luke 6:1–11; 11:14–12:2;
14:1–6; 18:31–34
John 5:16–18; 8–9;
11:46–57

**14. Transfigured**
Matthew 9:9–12; 10;
17:1–19
Mark 1:14–20; 3:13–19;
9:2–10
Luke 5:1–11; 6:12–16;
9:1–36

**15. Suffered**
Mark 14:17–15:20
Luke 22:39–23:25
John 13; 18:1–19:16

**16. Crucified**
Matthew 27:32–44
Mark 15:21–32
Luke 23:26–43
John 19:17–27

**17. Forsaken**
Matthew 27:45–56
Mark 15:33–41
Luke 23:44–49
John 19:28–37

**18. Risen**
Matthew 27:57–28:7
Mark 15:42–16:7
Luke 23:50–24:7
John 19:38–20:13

**19. Doubted**
Matthew 28:8–20
Mark 16:1–14
Luke 24:8–49
John 20:14–21:25

**20. Ascended**
Mark 16:19–20
Luke 24:50–53
Acts 1:1–11

**21. Waiting**
John 14:16–19, 26
15:26–27; 16:5–14
Acts 1:12–16

**22. Power**
Acts 1:5–8; 2:1–41

**23. Weakness**
Acts 2:42–9:31; 17–18;
21:27–28:31
2 Corinthians 1:3–11;
1:23–12:10

**24. Peace**
Romans 4:4–8, 25; 5:1–8

# Study Guide

**THIS SHORT STUDY GUIDE** is designed to help you discuss your thirty-day journey with a small group, meeting together over a period of six weeks. The questions will help you review and apply what you have learned.

You may find it helpful to begin each group meeting by sharing from the chapters you read:

- something new you discovered
- something that surprised you
- something you found hard to understand

## WEEK 1: READ CHAPTERS 1–5

1. How would you describe what the Bible is about? How is it relevant to your life today?

2. How does what happened in the Garden of Eden (chapter 2) help us to understand our world today?

3. Abraham worshiped idols until God appeared to him (chapter 3). How is the God of the Bible different from an idol?

4. Joseph said to his brothers, "You intended to harm me, but God intended it for good" (chapter 4). Think of a time when someone tried to make your life difficult. How did God use that experience for good?

5. God's presence came down to the tabernacle (chapter 5). Where should we look to find God's presence in the world today? Why?

## WEEK 2: READ CHAPTERS 6–9

1. What are the key qualities that we should look for in a leader (chapter 6)? Why?

2. What did God promise to do for David (chapter 7)? Why is this promise so important in the Bible story?

3. Why do you think God's people kept turning away from Him (chapter 8)? What causes people to turn away from God today?

4. Daniel and his friends were highly successful in Babylon (chapter 9). What are the greatest temptations for successful people today, and how can we overcome these temptations?

5. What does the Old Testament story tell us about the fundamental problems of the human race? What hope does the Old Testament offer?

## WEEK 3: READ CHAPTERS 10–15

1. What does the New Testament tell us about the birth of Jesus (chapter 10)? Why do you believe in the virgin birth, and if not, why not?

2. What are the biggest pressures that you face in your life? To what extent do you think Jesus can relate to these struggles (chapter 11)? Why?

3. Why were many people deeply opposed to Jesus (chapter 13)? What reasons might a person have for opposing Jesus today?

4. In what ways is Jesus like us? In what ways is He different from any other person who has ever lived (chapter 14)?

5. How would you explain the extreme cruelty and violence that was poured out on Jesus (chapter 15)? Why did Jesus not retaliate?

## WEEK 4: READ CHAPTERS 16–21

1. How would you describe the difference between the two thieves who were crucified next to Jesus (chapter 16)? How does Jesus' response to the thief give hope for us today?

2. Explain in your own words what happened during the three hours of darkness when Jesus was on the cross (chapter 17).

3. The New Testament teaches that Jesus rose from the dead (chapter 18). What difference does this make today for people who believe?

4. What significance do you see in the fact that the disciples were slow to believe that Jesus rose from the dead (chapter 19)?

5. Jesus has ascended to heaven and continues to bless His people (chapter 20). In what ways can you see God's blessing in your life today?

## WEEK 5: READ CHAPTERS 22–25

1. What do the miraculous events on the day of Pentecost teach us about what God wants to do through His people today (chapter 22)? To what extent do you see these things happening?

2. Think of a situation you have faced (or are facing) that caused you to feel completely overwhelmed. What have you seen God doing in your life through this experience of weakness (chapter 23)?

3. Is it possible to be sure that you have peace with God (chapter 24)? How could you know this?

4. God calls us to fight against the sin that lurks in our hearts (chapter 25). How would you go about fighting the power of pride, greed, or envy in your own life?

5. In what ways have these chapters caused you to adjust your expectations of the Christian life?

## WEEK 6: READ CHAPTERS 26–30

1. How would you try to help someone who said that he wanted to follow Jesus but was worried that he could not keep it up (chapter 26)?

2. Think about a situation of pain or loss in your life. How did God cause you to grow through that experience (chapter 27)?

3. If anyone is in Christ, he or she is a new creation (chapter 28). Do you believe that you are in Christ? If so, in what ways are you different from the person you would have been without Christ? If not, how do you think you would be different in Christ?

4. If you knew that you had one week left to live, what would your priorities be? How might your answer impact the way you live this week?

5. What is the most important thing you have learned from your thirty-day journey through the Bible? How would you like this to affect your life?

THE BEATITUDES ARE NOT TELLING YOU HOW TO
BECOME A CHRISTIAN—THEY TELL YOU WHAT A
TRUE CHRISTIAN LOOKS LIKE.

# GET THE RESOURCES YOU NEED FOR
# WHEN LIFE TAKES AN UNEXPECTED TURN.

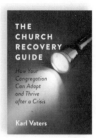

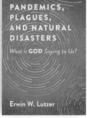
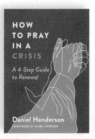